THIRTEEN MIRACLES

A NEUROSURGEON MEETS JESUS

DEAN C. LOHSE, MD

D1532478

To Harold and Junie Norris,
and Larry and Eunice Lohse,
who kept the faith through good times and bad,
and passed salvation to the generations that follow.

And to the preachers, evangelists and missionaries who bring order to worlds of chaos, love to hearts of hate, and light to nights of darkness.

INTRODUCTION

I felt the eyes of the circulating nurse boring into the back of my head. I swore I even felt her breath on the exposed bit of neck between my scrub shirt and the ill-fitting hood that covered my way-too-long hair, but that may have been my imagination. Her responsibility was to keep me from contaminating the surgical field, and since this was my first time scrubbed on a real operation, she knew it was a probability. On this craniotomy for a suspected brain abscess, I had already gone through two gowns and three pairs of surgical gloves just to semi-safely stand alongside the second assistant. Now, awkward and uncertain, with my hands in front of me—above my waist and below my mid-chest—I tried to touch nothing. Theoretically, I was learning about neurosurgery, but I longed to be invisible.

The year was 1973. The very earliest of CT scanners had not been built. For diagnosis we relied on history as provided by the patient and their family, a careful neurological examination, and primitive x-ray studies. Neurosurgeons made big incisions because localizing the lesion was uncertain. For a medical student who had learned anatomy mostly out of books, the surgical field was incomprehensible. I learned anatomy topside up and right-on-right, left-on-left. But when I stood at the top of the head, everything I had studied was upside down and backward. And that was only the part of the patient I could see. Except for the bloody patch of scalp and bone, everything was covered with green sheets.

Then, like the sunrise after a rainy night, it was suddenly there: the human brain, looking like the illustrations of Frank Netter, but even more stunning. Most things in anatomy class were the opposite: they looked better in the pictures. Since reality was usually disappointing, sometimes nauseating, I had not expected my breath to be taken away —but it was.

The surface of the brain glistened white, the tiny arteries brightly red and the larger veins blueberry blue, the whole mass pulsating gently with the heartbeat. This was the magic place where crude sensations turned into perceptions and biological impulses into thoughts, where dancers stored their steps and orators their words.

I may have gasped in wonder.

The attending doctor asked for the department chairman. They talked about how the width of one gyrus compared to another. After they reached a consensus, the attending passed a blunt metal tube into the surface of the brain and a wave of creamy pus squirted out, spilling over the brain's surface and onto the drapes. Apparently it was okay if the patient contaminated his own surgical field as long as I didn't do it. The pus was collected for laboratory samples, and the remainder discarded. The brain was washed with clear normal saline and became beautiful again, a small scar on the surface where the probe had drained the pus, but now no longer swollen. The danger of death had passed. The healing began.

And I was hooked.

There is no ignoble specialty in medicine, but none better than neurosurgery. Every organ has a critical function, but the brain is the most magical. I spent the next eight years of my life learning everything I could to become a full-fledged neurosurgeon, and another thirty years mastering new skills and adding new knowledge. I cannot imagine any other profession more satisfying. Nor can I imagine anything so challenging. It demanded all my intellect, drained all my emotions, and sucked up all my time.

Jesus healed men, women, and children during his ministry on Earth. Miracles we call them, and miracles they were. I envied him the seeming ease of laying on hands without a five-minute scrub and sterile gloves. He had no skin incisions to open and close, no x-rays to interpret, no staff to train, no drug side effects nor transfusion reactions.

Modern medicine in general and neurosurgery in particular is full of miracles. But there are extraordinary moments when something beyond known science is at work. I've been blessed to see a few of these moments, and I wanted to compare my experience with the historical record. I started with the Gospel of Matthew simply because it is the first in the New Testament. In several passages Jesus healed "many people," but Matthew also describes thirteen specific instances in which the details of a single individual's sickness and healing occur.

I found that not only did Jesus perform miracles in the first century AD; he heals today.

Matthew describes Jesus preaching, "Repent for the

kingdom of heaven has come near."[1] The words are simple, the message profound. Repent means simply to turn around or turn away. Turn away from ambition to wisdom, from lust to love, from anger to peace, from guilt and shame to acceptance and joy. Because the Kingdom of God is right here, an arm's length away from the truth that can set us free. This is the first message of the Gospel.

But then he calls the first four disciples; he resumes proclaiming the good news about the kingdom of heaven, but with one added twist: " . . . healing every disease and sickness among the people."[2]

Many times, I have brushed by these words, having heard them so often that they're like Muzak in my ears, ignored. Now I don't let familiarity numb me to the intimate connection between repentance, the good news about the kingdom of heaven, and physical healing. Every religion encourages repentance from their particular definition of sin in order to access their particular version of heaven, but outside of Christianity none make a direct connection to physical healing. Matthew recognizes that these are radically new and different words. Jesus's good news about the kingdom of heaven is not that it is *there* in some far-off future or post-death, but that it has *come near*—it is at hand for anyone who is willing to turn and look. The same is true about healing. Jesus's healing is physical relief here and now, not a mind-over-matter exercise or spiritual acceptance of suffering.

Matthew unpacks this in a measured approach. He doesn't try to explain; he only reports. He starts with the Sermon on the Mount, a long look at what Jesus means by "Repent, the kingdom of heaven is at hand," which turns the common values of the world upside down. (If you're not familiar with it, I highly recommend putting this book down right now and reading Matthew, chapters 5-7. They are totally life changing.) Immediately after, Matthew continues with what happened when Jesus stopped talking and started walking. And that is where we will begin.

MIRACLE #1
LEPERS

A man with leprosy came and knelt before him and said, "Lord, if you are willing, you can make me clean."

Matthew 8:2

Awoman who had both AIDS and hepatitis C came to me with a painful and disabling spinal condition. All other means of treatment had been exhausted. Her only chance for an improved life lay with a long and complicated spine operation. I suggested she do her best to live with the condition; she suggested suicide would be a better alternative. I reconsidered.

The day of the surgery came. I cautioned the OR staff about the added risk of HIV and hepatitis C. *Be aware and be careful*, I said. After the anesthesiologist put her to sleep, we positioned her on a special frame, prepped the skin, and draped the surgical field in the usual sterile fashion. I injected the planned skin incision with a dilute solution of epinephrine, a minor, even optional, preparation to theoretically decrease superficial bleeding. This was part of my routine, something I had done literally thousands of times. But this time, as I pulled the needle out, I accidentally stuck it into the thick muscle below my left thumb.

I pulled it out immediately. The pain was trivial, but the fear was significant. For a moment I froze as adrenaline pumped through my system. My instincts pushed for "fight or flight." But at that moment there was nothing to fight, and I could not flee from an anesthetized patient who had put her trust in me.

I did what surgeons always do. I discarded the needle, changed gloves, and forgot about the pain and fear. I continued the operation. Six hours later, the last staple closed the skin and the bandage was placed. The patient now back on the stretcher and awakened, I had to face the nagging pain in my palm and my growing fear of disability and death. I had to imagine AIDS and hepatitis in a whole new light, no longer as a theoretical risk but as a personal threat. I imagined the end of my career as a surgeon and calculated the risk of a sloppy kiss to my wife or my children.

I had touched the leper; I was unclean.

A man with leprosy came and knelt before him and said, "Lord, if you are willing, you can make me clean."
Jesus reached out his hand and touched the man. "I am willing," he said. "Be clean." Immediately the man was cured of his leprosy. Then Jesus said to him, "See that you don't tell anyone. But go show yourself to the priest and offer the gift Moses commanded, as a testimony to them." (Matt. 8:2-4)

. . .

T his leper wasn't supposed to be kneeling in front of Jesus. He didn't have the right. Lepers were supposed to stand at least ten paces away and shout, "Unclean!" to people who came near—first-century social distancing.

And Jesus wasn't supposed to touch him. Leprosy was the only clear contagion of the age. Though the germ theory of disease was still a couple of millennia in the future, society recognized that at least this one disease could be transmitted person to person. Once Jesus touched the leper, he was contaminated. At risk himself, he became a risk to the people around him. He became "unclean."

Imagine the outrage from the disciples when the leper kneeled within arm's reach. See them flinching when Jesus reached out his hand, maybe taking a step back themselves. Maybe they wondered if this was the end of a promising ministry of hope and God's love.

But the healing worked. Then Jesus said something else surprising: *don't tell anyone.* By going to the priest and offering a thanksgiving sacrifice, the outcast leper could follow a legal process to return to society. *Just do that and keep quiet*, Jesus told him, not like a person building a brand but giving a gift, private and simple—like love.

I once thought that the tradition of accepting personal risk for the benefit of the patient goes back to Hippocrates. But neither the Hippocratic Oath nor the Oath of Maimonides deals with risk to the physician. Over the centuries, plenty of physicians chose self-protection for very good reasons. Perhaps the tradition of taking personal risk goes back not to Hippocrates or Maimonides, but to the story of Jesus and the leper.

Jesus may have known the risk to himself would be low,

being God and all—but maybe not. It is not at all clear that he knew for certain what would happen next. In the Garden of Gethsemane, he begged his Father to allow a different future than the one he was facing. If he imagined other outcomes at that point, then he must have done the same three years before. When a leper kneeled at his feet, he wasn't sure what the impact would be; he only knew what his Father would have him do. He may have imagined touching the leper and pulling back a leprous hand. For just a moment, he may have envisioned the same thing I did when I stuck the needle in my hand: disease, a career falling away, isolation from loved ones.

The good news is that the leper was healed. My good news is that the woman's spine condition was cured by the surgery, and my subsequent HIV and Hepatitis C testing remained normal for the following year.

Matthew probably didn't include this healing account for the sole benefit of future health care providers. I faced a sick woman with HIV and hepatitis C, and I was afraid. But everyone faces lepers. It is hard to reach out to the homeless, the dirty, the criminals, the mentally ill, the drug addicts, and the alcoholics—the lepers of the twenty-first century. We are afraid.

But when that one guy with leprosy knelt down in front of Jesus, he reached out and touched him. And the world changed.

MIRACLE #2

THE CENTURION'S SERVANT AND AMAZING JESUS

When Jesus had entered Capernaum, a centurion came to him,
asking for help. "Lord," he said, "my servant lies at home
paralyzed, suffering terribly."

Matthew 8:5

The July day was hot, the water of Black Creek cool. The 26-year-old man was an accomplished water skier, so accomplished that he could ski barefoot, which required a boat speed of nearly 40 mph. He doesn't remember what made him fall. He remembers only floating on his back, cold water, blue sky, and fluffy white clouds above. His neck hurt, and he could not move at all, not even to lift his ears out of the water. But he did hear the whine of the approaching boat engine and felt the strong arms of his friends pull him out of the water.

Thirty minutes to the boat ramp, five minutes to call rescue, thirty minutes for the nearest ambulance to arrive, ten minutes to assess his condition and load into the ambulance, thirty minutes to the nearest hospital, ten minutes for initial assessment, ten minutes for initial x-rays, five minutes to reassess and call the neurosurgeon, and thirty minutes more for the neurosurgeon to arrive.

One hundred and sixty-five minutes, nearly three hours after a dislocation of the fifth and sixth cervical vertebrae had squashed his spinal cord, we met for the first time. He had good strength—great strength really—in his deltoids, weak biceps, and no movement in his triceps, hands, or legs. His anal sphincter was likewise flaccid. With his inability to move or shiver, his wet body lost heat in the air-conditioned ER, his body temperature already down to 96^0F.

By the time I got the history of the accident, the information from the exam, and the x-rays, another fifteen minutes or more had passed, now over three hours total.

The human spinal cord is a frail thing, no bigger around than the little finger on a small hand. The neurons and axons the consistency of Jell-O, its form is maintained only by tissue so thin you can see through it. Protection comes from the sheath of spinal fluid inside the spinal canal of the bony vertebrae. But once that bony canal is compromised, the cord is irretrievably injured by the smallest trauma.

Sometimes, if the compression has occurred gradually over a period of weeks or months, or if the cord compression has been quite brief like a quick bruise, the cord can recover, and the person can walk. But the water skier had sudden and severe cord compression for more than three hours. He had little hope.

His friends must have suspected this. The EMTs who transported him must have been more certain. The ER staff who did the initial evaluation understood that patients with severe spinal cord injuries didn't walk again. I knew for certain that a three-hour delay between injury and treatment time made the prognosis even worse.

Using cervical traction to realign the spine and relieve pressure on the cord was the protocol. This involved screwing steel tongs into the skull and then connecting the tongs to a rope through a pulley and, finally, to weights. The starting weight was 20 pounds; the protocol entailed a check and x-ray at that point, then a weight increase of 10-pound increments until the bones realigned. Sometimes the weights could go as high as 70-to-90 pounds before realignment occurred. But sometimes, if the ligamentous injury was severe, distraction and stretching of the already-damaged cord might occur at as little as 30 pounds.

Since the water skier had a very muscular neck and time was critical, I started at 30 pounds and went quickly to 50 and 70 with no success. Each weight increase was followed by a portable x-ray that took nearly fifteen minutes: position for the film cassette, the x-ray itself, transport to the radiology department for development, and return of the x-ray to the ER. Four hours had passed. And I was out of weights.

Now desperate, I turned to the unconventional. I gave him an intravenous dose of morphine and diazepam (Valium) and took hold of his head, one hand on each side of his jaw and the skull behind each ear. Then slowly, while mentally visualizing the spine, I pulled. And I said a little prayer.

I felt his neck muscles relax slightly, then a small movement, then a click. Nearly unconscious from the sedation, the water skier let out a sound like *ahh*. I let go of his head. In a moment he opened his eyes and spoke.

"I can feel my fingers," he said. "I think I can move my toes."

Phantom sensations are not uncommon after spinal cord

injuries, so my initial reaction was muted. But careful re-examination showed that he indeed could feel sensation in his hands and move his toes.

"Thank God," I said to myself.

But I should have been more literal and sincere. Maybe I should have said it aloud. The story of his recovery is too long to recount here, but though he never returned to water skiing and felt awkward if he tried to run, he had no pain, could walk and use his hands, and only the most careful neurologic exam could detect traces of his prior injury. He had been healed at that moment.

W*hen Jesus had entered Capernaum, a centurion came to him, asking for help.*

"Lord," he said, "my servant lies at home paralyzed, suffering terribly."

Jesus said to him, "Shall I come and heal him?"

The centurion replied, "Lord, I do not deserve to have you come under my roof. But just say the word, and my servant will be healed. For I myself am a man under authority, with soldiers under me. I tell this one, 'Go,' and he goes; and that one, 'Come,' and he comes. I say to my servant, 'Do this,' and he does it."

When Jesus heard this, he was amazed and said to those following him, "Truly I tell you that many will come from the east and the west, and will take their places at the feast with Abraham, Isaac, and Jacob in the kingdom of heaven. But the subjects of the kingdom will be thrown outside into the darkness, where there will be weeping and gnashing of teeth."

Then Jesus said to the centurion, "Go! Let it be done just as you believed it would." And his servant was healed at that moment (Matt. 8:5-13).

. . .

The centurion's servant "suffered greatly," but he was not the one who asked for help. The water skier "suffered greatly," but he couldn't ask for help. Sometimes in our moment of greatest suffering, greatest need, we are unable or unwilling to ask for help. We need a friend.

Our friend needs two things. The first is compassion. He/she needs to recognize great suffering. In the case of sudden and complete paralysis this is not too difficult. But sometimes our greatest suffering is less visible. Only our best friends see our invisible pain.

The other part of compassion, what sets it apart from sensitivity and sympathy, is the willingness to pay a certain price to relieve the pain. Quite understandably, the boating buddies quit skiing and headed for the boat ramp; we would have thought them callous or even criminal had they done anything less.

But the centurion had a servant, presumably a slave, a replaceable human being in those hard pre-Christian times. Presumably he had to walk from his garrison, most likely at Tiberius, to Capernaum, a distance of at least eight miles each way, an all-day journey. And he had to cross political, class, and racial barriers as well.

He could only do this if he had the second thing our friend in our greatest need must possess: faith.

The water skiers, the EMTs, and even the ER doctors, didn't have faith in me, the neurosurgeon, but they trusted a system. They didn't need to cross political, class, and racial barriers; they just needed to call 911.

The centurion, though, had to risk embarrassment, career setback, and physical harm to take a chance on the rumors about a Jewish mystic in the next town. He did something that no other person in the Bible ever did. He amazed God.

Jesus's answer recognized compassion and faith as means to reconciliation with God. Race doesn't count, religion doesn't count, location doesn't count—"*. . . many will come from the east and the west, and will take their place at the feast with Abraham, Isaac, and Jacob in the kingdom of heaven . . .*"

We Christians are fond of quoting the gospel John, 14:6. *Jesus answered, "I am the way, the truth, and the life. No one comes to the Father except through me."*

But I think we would be wise to remember Jesus's words in Matthew as well. People will come from the east and the west to feast in the kingdom of heaven. What those people demonstrate is compassion for servants who suffer greatly, and faith to walk all day at whatever personal cost to seek the healing power of God. That's what coming to the Father through Jesus looks like. That's what amazes God.

3

MIRACLE #3
FEVER AT HOME

*When Jesus came into Peter's house, he saw
Peter's mother-in-law lying in bed with a fever.*

Matthew 8:14

At some construction sites in Florida, contractors show up with a cooler of beer and a satchel of cash on Friday afternoons. They give their Mexican construction workers a couple of cold ones and their weekly salary. Soon afterward the workers send some money home and often celebrate with more beer. Sometimes they fight.

On a Friday night, a young worker named Javier had taken a baseball bat to the skull around midnight. The bar called 911. He and his co-workers wouldn't have called themselves. They would have rathered risk death than deportation.

While Javier had been drinking beer, I had been

anxiously packing two large bags. One bag held my back-pack with camping supplies; the other was filled with medicines, bandages, and a few simple surgical tools. After my night on call, I would be leaving for Central America where my team would travel to the end of the road, then up the Coen River in canoes. After that, we would hike for a day through the jungle to a remote village, where we planned to hold a medical clinic for three days. Resupply would be impossible. If I forgot something, someone might suffer because of my thoughtlessness.

Finally satisfied, I crawled into bed and tried to sleep. Lists of supplies and plane schedules kept driving peaceful slumber away. Finally I dozed off only to be woken a few minutes later by a call from the ER about Javier.

He had an open depressed skull fracture—in other words, a large laceration on his scalp with fragments of bone driven into his brain. And he was drunk, had no family in the USA, spoke no English, and had no health insurance.

An hour or so after the initial phone call, Javier and I were in surgery together. With the help of anesthesia, he slept, and with the help of stale coffee, I did not. The stress of the coming trip weighed on me along with the usual stress of a mutilated skull and a lacerated brain.

After a couple hours, I had removed the bone fragments, debrided and cleaned the injuries to the brain, and repaired the covering of the brain, the *dura mater*. The only essential part of the operation left to perform was the closure of the skin, and although the laceration had left ragged and irregular flaps, it required only lots of stitches, no skin grafts. I could relax.

A decision had to be made, though. The fracture had left a gaping hole in Javier's skull. One common way of handling this would be to simply close the skin and bring the patient back a few weeks later to put in an artificial plate. This method had the advantage of a lowered infection risk and, pertinent to me at this moment, a shorter operation.

I looked at the clock—3:30 a.m.

Now that I wasn't worried that Javier would die or be disabled, my adrenaline ebbed enough for me to shift from anxiety to anger. Not really at Javier—he wanted to be here even less than I did—but at the whole situation. I was tired and would get nothing but more tired. I might forget something vital for the mission trip, and I couldn't see a time in the next few days when I could catch up on sleep. Chronic sleep deprivation was a familiar misery, but misery nonetheless.

Javier, however, wasn't the kind of guy who would recover in a protected environment and return for an elective operation. He could be drinking beer next weekend, maybe having another fight and getting hit in the head again, this time without the protection of a large section of skull.

With a big sigh, I asked the OR crew to get the cranial reconstruction supplies and instruments. A plate could be fashioned out of a special metal alloy and fixed in place with many tiny screws. The process was tedious but not difficult, and when Javier woke up his skull would be just as tough as it had been before the fight.

As I started to work, I started to pray. *Thanks for pulling Javier through and all,* I told God, *but I'm angry to be here and wish you'd found some other way.*

Sometimes, not often, God talks back when I pray. This was one of those times.

God: "Why is it that you're angry?"

Me: "Because I'm going to be tired and miserable. I have a plane to catch in the morning."

God: "And where is it that you're going?"

Me: "Well, in case you've forgotten, I'm going on a mission trip for *you.*"

God: "And what exactly do you think you'll be doing for me?"

Me: "I'm going to be giving medical care to poor people who don't have anybody else to do it. And they don't even speak English."

God: "Uh-huh."

W hen Jesus came into Peter's house, he saw Peter's mother-in-law lying in bed with a fever. He touched her hand and the fever left her, and she got up and began to wait on him.

When evening came, many who were demon possessed were brought to him, and he drove out the spirits with a word and healed all the sick (Matt. 8:14-16).

M issions begin at home. Jesus's friend's mother-in-law was sick. In the first century AD — before diagnostic tools (even thermometers), acetaminophen, antibiotics, or sterile surgical technique—a fever was a life-threatening condition. Never mind that the courtyard was filling with the demon-possessed. Never mind that sick people filled the streets of that little town. Mom was sick. Jesus's first priority was to touch and relieve her fever.

I had failed to remember (again) that God could heal Javier or an entire village in Central America without any help from me. Sometimes, when I surrender to his will, he lets me help.

But whatever gifts I might have to heal, to spread light and salt in the world, I need to use at home first. First, I need to take care of whoever is in front of me—my mother, my wife, my children and grandchildren. First, I need to take care of the drunk, illegal immigrant with the skull fracture.

Jesus heals one person at a time. Matthew tells us that "many" who were demon possessed came that evening, but we get the impression that Jesus met them one at a time, and gave each the word that set them free. He didn't wave his arm over the front yard and everyone went away happy, although his godly healing powers would have made that possible.

He healed one person at a time; I had to do the same. Javier was my patient at that moment, and I was not to be distracted by my mission to help a village a thousand miles away.

Also, Jesus didn't seem to react to crowds. He reacted to individual suffering. I find it easy to believe that God is so big that he can't possibly be interested in me, one of eight billion humans on our little planet in a big universe, much less worry whether I have a fever or not. But Jesus shows us that he is not only God of the very big; he is God of the very small. He notices and cares about my fevers, and my demons.

When Matthew told us about the previous two healings, he didn't reveal what either the leper or the centurion's servant did next. In this story, though, he tells us, " . . . she got up and began to wait on him." Maybe she cooked dinner or did the dishes. Maybe she mended his clothes or washed his feet. Or maybe she organized the demon-possessed in the front yard—that would have taken some motherly strength and persuasion!

But even if she felt well, she had no such obligation. As a

senior member of a household in a society that reveres the elderly, Peter's mother-in-law did not have to serve anyone, whether she had a fever or not. After her fever abated, she could have come out for some polite conversation and a glass of wine, watched the sunset, and gone back to bed.

But she didn't.

I've seen lots of different responses in people who have recovered from a life-threatening illness. Some lapse into a long and deep depression. Some become overly anxious about their health, controlling diet and exercise, adding supplemental nutrients or vitamins, and avoiding suspected contaminants in food, air, and water. Some become hyperactive, fulfilling a "bucket list" of experiences and pleasures.

Others make peace with those who are angry, apologize to those they have wronged, give generously to those in need, and encourage those who are struggling. Sometimes they go on mission trips. These are the ones I admire, the ones like Peter's mother-in-law—the ones who "got up and began to wait on him."

4

MIRACLE #4

DEMONS

When he arrived at the other side in the region of the Gadarenes,
two demon-possessed men came from the tombs to meet him.
They were so violent that no one could pass that way.

Matthew 8:28

In 1999, I found myself in a small Central American village, the only doctor anyone had ever seen. This was my first overseas trip as a medical missionary. Much prayer and persuasion from trusted advisors had convinced me to travel this far from my comfort zone. The village was a four-hour canoe ride and a one-hour hike from the nearest road, and no one spoke English.

Fortunately I had at my side John Whited, the resident missionary to the Bribri tribe, and Penny Velie, a nurse with mission experience. John translated, and Penny guided me. We saw about eighty patients the first day, mostly with conditions that rapidly became familiar: water-borne GI diseases, vitamin deficiencies, intestinal parasites. One boy had a heart murmur; one teen-age girl wanted to know when her baby would come. Gradually I became comfortable in my role, even grateful for the privilege to be there. One boy couldn't see things close up, and my glasses seemed to help him. Since I'd brought a spare pair, I gave him mine.

While we saw patients, some of our team members gave testimonies and gospel presentations in the waiting room. Much discussion ensued, but many people became excited at the Good News and were eager to embrace and explore this new worship.

Only one man seemed to have a puzzling request. He came early in the morning, before we were ready to see patients. He complained that something sharp had pierced his right arm, and it wouldn't come out. I looked carefully at the arm and found absolutely nothing, so I reassured him the best I could and sent him on his way. He didn't come back during the regular clinic hours.

After the patients had gone home, night fell hard and fast, the darkness deep under the jungle canopy. We cocooned ourselves inside the unfinished schoolhouse by sheathing the interior with a giant mosquito net hung from the rafters, the space lit by candles and a gas lantern. There we cooked a simple meal and, exhausted, spread out sleeping mats and prepared to rest. Penny took a sleeping pill and was out cold before anyone else had lain down.

Then we had visitors. One man who had heard the Gospel was so excited that he told his neighbor, a man who had moved from the outside a few years before and married a village woman. The woman had recently died of cancer, and her husband was now alone. The neighbor agreed reluctantly to make his way through the dark to hear the message.

The five of us who were still awake met with them. As we were introduced, I realized the neighbor was the same dark-skinned man who had the mysterious and invisible arm injury.

We listened to the man's story. He was a native of Haiti and had joined a cult that worshipped the devil. He had progressed to the fifth of seven training levels to become a satanic priest when he became frightened and fled the country. He took the first ship out, to Limon, Costa Rica, and continued to flee until he was well beyond the nearest road. There, in this village, he had settled down and gotten married, hoping to have outrun his demons.

Our team presented the gospel to him, and he seemed to be on the verge of accepting. But he was afraid. Something inside from his prior training held him in fear. Unable to accept salvation, he asked us to pray for him.

We laid hands on him, and I was overcome to the point of obsession with casting out his demon. I wasn't even sure I believed in demons and certainly had never witnessed an exorcism. Yet that's what I prayed for, but in English, so I'm sure he didn't understand me.

Then we opened our eyes. He quivered under our hands, his eyelids fluttered, and he opened his eyes and grinned. Full of joy, he told us he had been set free, asked for one of our Spanish-translation Bibles, and received Jesus. A half-hour later, we sent them off into the darkness with one of our flashlights.

One member of our team, Jim Young, said we should pray for protection because whenever a demon is driven out it looks for a new home. But before we could pray, John's wife, Daisy, suddenly convulsed and lay on the ground shaking uncontrollably. I examined her, and clinically would call the condition a pseudo-seizure. The four of us still conscious laid hands on her, praying for her deliverance and protection for all of us.

Daisy sat up, a bit confused but seemingly unaffected and at peace. Then we all went to our corners of the cocoon, turned off the lights, and tried to sleep. I lay there in the darkness asking myself if that had really just happened.

The morning we left, the newly delivered demon-possessed Haitian came to see us off. He no longer complained about mysterious pains and appeared to be filled with joy.

After the mission trip, I had only distant contact with Penny. I heard that she had developed some health issues and had gone out on disability. I didn't know the full story until recently. This is her story in her words:

I was zonked out on zolpidem during that encounter with the late night visitor and demonic attack. But during the night I woke up with "urgency and burning" typical for a urinary tract infection. I'd had similar infections before so I didn't think much of it; I had brought with me my usual antibiotic and started it immediately. By the end of the week when we had returned to the states, the bladder infection got much worse. I called my urologist, and he changed the antibiotic. But again the infection did not get better. For four months I took one antibiotic after another but by then I was peeing mostly blood, and the pain was excruciating. My urologist finally did a cystoscopy and discovered hundreds of Hunner's ulcers in my bladder, bloody little ulcers found in patients with interstitial cystitis.

I needed morphine patches daily to control the pain and still *needed Percocet for breakthrough. Some days the pain was bad enough that I needed a wheelchair.*

I stopped taking teams on the mission field. Two years later, with continued pain and disability, my urologist offered me the most radical solution: complete removal of my bladder. I was so desperate for relief, I agreed.

Then, one week before the procedure was scheduled, a couple from my church, Dr. David Friedline and his wife Delores, were hosting a pastor from Africa who specialized in deliverance from demonic attacks. They invited me to come to their house to meet him. I told this African pastor about the Costa Rica trip and how sick I was when I returned home, that I was not able to take missions teams overseas. I said nothing about demons. Remember, I hadn't even been awake during the encounter.

The pastor said he had "read my mail" and felt the presence of the demonic at our first introduction. He prayed, rebuked the devil. Over the next few hours and days, I started feeling better. I cancelled my bladder surgery. It was not an instant healing; I had to walk it out for another year.

But a year later, instead of being wheelchair bound without a bladder, I was off narcotics and able to start going on mission trips again. I have been to Kenya, Uganda, China, and Inner Mongolia.

So that night in Costa Rica, that encounter with evil, even though—or maybe because—I was asleep, had a profound effect on my life.

Until that night in a small village deep in the jungles of Central America, I didn't believe in demons or demon possession. And I suppose all of the events I describe above can be re-phrased in modern psychological-medical language to convey the same events.

But the simplest explanations are usually the best. So let's look at this story with the understanding that demons are real then and now.

When he arrived at the other side in the region of the Gadarenes, two demon-possessed men came from the tombs to meet him. They were so violent that no one could pass that way. "What do you want with us, Son of God?" they shouted. "Have you come here to torture us before the appointed time?"

Some distance away from them a large herd of pigs was feeding. The demons begged Jesus, "If you drive us out, send us into the herd of pigs."

He said to them, "Go!" So they came out and went into the pigs, and the whole herd rushed down the steep bank into the lake and died in the water. Those tending the pigs ran off, went into the town and reported all this, including what had happened to the demon-possessed men. Then the whole town went out to meet Jesus. And when they saw him, they pleaded with him to leave their region (Matt. 8:28-34).

Imagine crossing from Florida to the Bahamas by boat, the trip marked by a life-threatening tropical storm, and reaching dry land with a sense of relief and thanksgiving. But then you are met by two maniacs running from the cemetery, screaming something about "Son of God, torture, and the appointed time."

You look around for help and all you see are a couple of pig farmers who are busy trying to distance themselves and their pigs from you and the screaming maniacs. They've seen this before, and it hasn't ended well. You're with your new best friend, Jesus, who says amazing things about the kingdom of heaven being right here, at hand, and you want to believe him. But so far he has shown no proper fear of contagious disease, occupying military powers, or storms at sea. Those things turned out all right so far, but maybe he's just lucky. It's hard to trust his judgment. Now, facing madness, what will he do?

The men are possessed by demons—that much is clear. And they are strong; otherwise someone would have locked them up or chained them where they wouldn't bother people. But that is all that is clear.

Why do they call Jesus "Son of God?" Could it be true? Is he really the Messiah? You may have wondered in silence. He certainly hasn't claimed it, not yet.

And, if the demons are afraid of torture, why do they run toward Jesus instead of away? Is there something left in the possessed men that brings their feet toward Jesus while their demons beg for mercy?

And what could possibly torture a demon? Could it be courage, freedom from earthly concerns, trust in God, pure righteousness? Could the appointed time be the death of the men they possess? Is that when they are condemned to hell?

The demons make a strange conditional request. *If* Jesus decides to throw them out of the men—this event is not apparently inevitable—then they want to go into the herd of pigs, dumb creatures that would not even be kosher food for Jesus and his friends. The only connection with the men who are possessed and the pigs is that men living in a cemetery and pigs are both unclean by Jewish custom and law.

So far, the demons have done all the talking.

Then Jesus says one word: "Go."

And the strangest thing happens. The maniacs become

peaceful and the pigs become agitated—so agitated that they run into the sea and drown.

Jesus still isn't talking, but the town hears about the pig stampede, comes out to see Jesus, and finds the maniacs clothed and in their right minds. You might think this would be a good thing—the lost among them had been restored, and they could bury their dead in the cemetery again. This might be a good tradeoff for a bunch of lost pigs.

But, no, they were afraid. Because who could drive out demons except the prince of demons? Maybe they figured the demons they knew were better than the demons they didn't. The safe thing would be to send the Jews back home and start raising more pigs. So Jesus left. And the only ones any richer were the two men who had lived in the cemetery with the demons.

So what can we learn from all this?

First, we don't understand demons. Sometimes they come from exposure to devil worship; sometimes they are manifested by otherwise inexplicable mental illness or medical conditions.

Second, demons can possess us. When possessed, we become unable to control our feelings and behavior. We are not our best self.

Third, we can't exorcise our own demons. We need someone to pray for us.

Fourth, demons are tortured by courage and faithfulness.

Fifth, demons prefer to go somewhere else, someplace unclean, maybe into someone who is tired and weak and afraid.

Sixth, demons cannot separate us from the love of God. About thirty years after Jesus visited the Gadarenes, St. Paul addressed this in a letter to the nascent church in Rome:

. . .

...**N**either death nor life...nor **demons**...nor anything else in all creation, will be able to separate us from the love of God that is in Christ Jesus our Lord (Rom. 8: 38-39).

Jesus will cross the sea to find you and send your demons away.

5

MIRACLE #5

THE SINS OF THE SICK

Jesus stepped into a boat, crossed over and came to his own town.
Some men brought to him a paralyzed man, lying on a mat.

Matthew 9:1

The boy's mother was in her mid-thirties, but not likely to see her forties without a miracle. She had been a hard drinker and user of multiple non-prescription drugs, and now, though her demons were at bay, her bone marrow and liver were failing rapidly. Her four girlfriends were her strength, a liver transplant was her hope, and her teen-age son was her joy.

But that day her time had run out. Due to lack of platelets from her depleted bone marrow and lack of coagulation factors from her diseased liver, she suffered spontaneous intracranial bleeding and hovered in a coma, nearing death. An operation and another miracle would be needed to get her to that liver transplant.

A former nurse, now administrator in charge of risk management and miscellaneous tasks, called me and told me about the situation. Since the patient had no next-of-kin of legal age, an administrative consent had been obtained for surgery. Though I didn't legally have to do it, the administrator asked if I would speak with the son, a fourteen-year-old who had been in foster care for most of his life. Only in the past year had he and his mother been able to reunite.

I explained the situation to him as well as I could, trying to cushion him for more bad news that would likely follow. I finished, and for a moment the three of us stood silently in the ICU hallway outside his unconscious mother's room.

Then he looked me square in the eye and said, "Are you any good?"

The nurse-administrator gasped and started to say something. I stopped her. He was only asking what everybody wanted to know but didn't dare ask.

I was good, but I wasn't God. "I think so," I said, holding his gaze. "But the problem is bigger than my skills. No matter how well her surgery goes, she needs to stop bleeding and heal from the surgery, and that may not happen."

He nodded once, looked into his mother's room, nodded one more time, and walked away. I felt neither blessed nor cursed, only inadequate.

I saw him two more times, once a few hours later to tell him the surgery went well, and again a few days later when, from liver failure and re-bleeding, she died.

I wished I could do for his mother what Jesus could do: forgive sins, absolve her of all consequences of her sins, and give her back her life.

· · ·

*J*esus *stepped into a boat, crossed over and came to his own town. Some men brought to him a paralyzed man, lying on a mat. When Jesus saw their faith, he said to the man, "Take heart, son; your sins are forgiven." At this, some of the teachers of the law said to themselves, "This fellow is blaspheming!"* (Matt. 9:1-3)

Someone always objects to the forgiveness of sins. We demand accountability. Actions have consequences. This is how the world works, and it is what we teach our children.

We like to think our sins are choices. But most of us adults know that it is more complicated than that. Often the initial sin is trivial. Maybe the woman in my story was a teen-ager with a friend who wanted to try whiskey just to find out what the big deal was, and one drink was all it took to start a lifelong addiction impossible to beat. We make decisions because of our addictions and compulsions as well as our allegiances to friends and family. Consequently, our decision to sin doesn't seem like a choice at all. We do what we have to do.

A few years ago, a car pulled up to the ER and someone shoved the rear seat passenger out onto the pavement and sped away. The deserted friend was dirty, bruised all over, and a little drunk, but not enough to explain the depth of his coma. Labs showed the liver profile and suppressed bone marrow of chronic alcoholism, and a CT scan showed an acute subdural hematoma.

The hospital staff replaced coagulation factors and platelets with blood bank plasma, and I rushed him to the operating room. The depth of his coma was such that I did not really expect survival, especially with the liver and bone marrow issues, but without any family to give or deny permission to proceed, I wanted to err on the side of the most aggressive treatment.

As soon as the scalp was shaved I could see evidence of previous brain surgery, perhaps for another alcohol-related head injury. This made me even more pessimistic about a good neurologic recovery even if he did survive.

The surgery went as well as could be expected. The hematoma was removed and the bleeding stopped. I closed the wound, sent him to the ICU on a respirator, and went to the surgical waiting room to see if any family had materialized.

His mother was waiting alone. Far from distressed, she took in my account stoically, told me that he had indeed suffered another serious alcohol-related head injury several years prior in Baltimore, and that he had left her house four days before without leaving a note or calling.

I told her that her son remained in a coma, on a respirator, and survival chances were less than 50-50. She nodded once, visited her son for less than five minutes, and went home.

The following morning I was pleasantly surprised to find the man had improved dramatically from his pre-op status. He breathed weakly on his own, moved all his extremities purposefully, and his brainstem reflexes had returned. Although he did not respond to voice requests or commands, and therefore was technically still in coma, this was a level of coma from which patients often recovered. Feeling optimistic I looked over the rest of his labs and found the only immediately life-threatening condition to be severe anemia—a not unexpected finding given the surgical blood loss and the state of his bone marrow. I ordered a transfusion and went to look for his mother to tell her the good news.

She wasn't in the waiting room, so I decided I'd call her later if she hadn't shown up by the time I planned to leave the hospital. Just then I got a page from the nurse. We couldn't proceed with the transfusion because the mother refused permission.

I told the nurse not to worry; I would talk to the mother. She undoubtedly thought the situation was still as grim as it had seemed the night before and didn't want unnecessary transfusions if he wasn't going to survive anyway.

I met the mother outside the ICU and gave her the good news. Her son, who we thought was dead, looked like he would live, and early signs pointed to a good quality of life. This is the kind of news neurosurgeons like to give.

Much to my surprise, she told me she understood perfectly. She explained, "I told him that if he drank again I would do nothing to help him."

"But it's only a transfusion," I said, still not under-standing.

"Not only will I not consent to the transfusion, I want him off the respirator."

"But he'll die," I said.

"Exactly," she said. "He's been trying to kill himself for years. He has been in and out of rehab—four inpatient stays for a month each time—and one major head injury ten years ago. What happened this time was inevitable. If he survives, he'll do it again."

Her mind was made up, and she had power of attorney and next-of-kin authority to decide her son's fate. Yet, it seemed wrong. I contacted the intensive care specialist in charge of the respirator and told him the situation. He met with the mother, but he also point-blank refused to discontinue the respirator. The compromise was an emergency meeting of the Ethics Committee.

The committee is made up of the hospital chaplain, the risk-management administrator, the director of the ICU, and a couple more doctors experienced in end-of-life decisions. The next morning she faced them down. I'll never forget what she said.

She explained in graphic detail the twenty-plus-year battle with alcoholism, and all the treatment failures. "He has a terminal disease," she concluded. "If he had cancer instead of alcoholism, you wouldn't hesitate to honor my request. His alcoholism is his terminal disease."

Her logic was irrefutable. I didn't want to do what she requested, but she had the legal authority, and I didn't have to live with her son through his recovery. We discontinued the respirator, and he never got the blood transfusion or any other extraordinary treatments beyond fluids, nutrition, and comfort medications.

But even though the Ethics Committee had not come to the conclusion I wanted, the meeting had bought a few hours of recovery time. By then he had woken from his coma and recovered sufficiently to survive off the respirator. The transfusion would have certainly made his recovery quicker, but he survived without it. A few days later he went home. With his mother.

"Which is easier: to say, 'Your sins are forgiven' or to say, 'Get up and walk?' But I want you to know that the Son of Man has authority on earth to forgive sins." So he said to the paralyzed man, "Get up, take your mat and go home." Then the man got up and went home. When the crowd saw this, they were filled with awe; and *they praised God, who had given such authority to man* (Matt. 9:4-8).

Τhe people at Peter's house saw the paralyzed man get up and go home. But what awed them was not only the recovery of his physical ability, but that his sins had been forgiven. They praised God, because if there had been mercy for this paralyzed man, maybe there was mercy for them, too. Maybe they could be freed from whatever sins bound them. God had come down and given such authority to man.

My patient didn't return for post-op appointments. I never learned the end of the story. I like to imagine that the young man was finally freed from his alcoholism and that he and his mother lived happily ever after. Maybe. That would be awesome.

All I know is that it is possible. While my particular habitual sin hadn't ruined my liver and bone marrow, it had wrecked the most precious relationship in my life. I couldn't fix it by just trying to be better. I had tried—four times, forty times, four hundred times? I lost count. But when I was helpless, Jesus talked to me, told me to trust him, and sent me home. He removed from me the burden of habitual sin, and he fixed the relationships that I had so nearly destroyed. This is the power of the forgiveness of sins.

Jesus doesn't care if you've been through rehab four times or forty or four hundred. He is always willing to forgive your sins, whatever they are. And you will want to pick up your mat and follow him. He will take you home.

That is awesome.

6

MIRACLE #6
BLEEDING ALONE

Just then a woman who had been subject to bleeding for twelve years came up behind him and touched the edge of his cloak. She said to herself, "If only I touch his cloak, I will be healed." Jesus turned and saw her. "Take heart, daughter," he said, "your faith has healed you." And the woman was healed at that moment.

Matthew 9:20-22

We think we've heard about "faith healing" before, but we haven't. He told the leper, "Be clean," and he was. He commended the faith of the centurion, but the faith of the centurion's servant wasn't mentioned. Peter's mother-in-law just had to be in the house. The two Gadarene men were dispossessed of demons without any mention of faith. The paralyzed man, faithful or not, had his sins forgiven.

But now Jesus tells this woman, " . . .*your faith has healed you.*"

This has been a stumbling block for me. It goes against my midwestern, German-Norwegian heritage of hard work, stoicism, and perseverance. We don't whine about problems impossible to fix; we soldier on. It also goes against my scientific training and medical experience. The menor-rhagia this woman suffered from is caused by endocrine imbalances, gynecological neoplasms, coagulation disorders —not by lack of faith.

Debbie was a 27-year-old dental hygienist who came to see me because she was quite sure that she must have had a slipped disk—her left leg wasn't working right. Bright and cheery with a ready and perfect smile, she told me her friends had gotten weak legs from slipped disks. She needed it fixed quickly; between her job and two small children she couldn't afford to be slowed by a clumsy leg. The first symp-toms started three weeks before and now seemed worse.

Debbie seemed like the type of patient I loved to see—a happy, young woman with what sounded like an easily solv-able problem. Yet something nagged at me even before I examined her. No pain. No apparent distress. Although back injuries such as a slipped (herniated) disk could happen without pain, such cases were exceedingly rare, occurring only in very stoic individuals, in very severe disk herniation when the nerve damage also damages the pain fibers, or, even more rarely, in patients with the congenital absence of pain. None of these situations seemed to fit Debbie.

I examined her and found that although what she had noted about her left leg was true—loss of coordination—she had ignored or not noticed the loss of coordination in her left arm as well. Her reflex pattern pointed to a problem in her brain, not her spine.

One of the hard things about being a neurosurgeon is bringing bad news. Few gentle ways are there to say, "It's not a slipped disk. You have a brain tumor."

What I told Debbie: "We need to rule out another problem first. I'll arrange a CT scan of your head today." The small comfort of "rule out" balances the terror of "another problem" and "CT scan of head."

A few days later Debbie had surgery for a glioblastoma in her right cerebrum. The surgery went as well as surgery for a malignant tumor can go—no worsening of her weakness, no dangerous brain swelling, no infections. Everything was good except the prognosis: roughly a year to live, with radiation and chemotherapy.

The day after I gave her the prognosis and told her about treatment options, I entered her hospital room as a Baptist minister was leaving. I had the feeling that I had come close to interrupting a prayer. His card and a New Testament lay on the tray-table. *Good for her*, I thought. *Time to be prepared for heaven.* And perhaps a community of good-hearted people would surround her family in their time of need.

As the months went by Debbie lost her hair and her cheery disposition. Although always polite, she became a stoic warrior. Complications due to her treatments led to hospitalizations for bone marrow suppression and consequent infections. Her left-sided coordination problems progressed to disabling hemiplegia.

As medical miracles failed her, she turned to religion. A new Bible and Christian books appeared on her bedside table. Gospel music played from the radio. The television broadcast evangelist sermons. More cards from more clergymen appeared at her bedside.

She lost the ability to speak. I came by to see her each

day she was on the oncology ward. Lacking any material skills to help, I held her hand for a few moments before moving on. Sometimes she would meet my eyes, sometimes not.

One day near the end, I held her hand and let my emotions wash over me: sadness, anger at her disease, frustration at my own ability to have so little impact on her outcome, and all the feelings that are conjured by helplessness in the face of cosmic injustice. Her eyes were closed, her expression pained. I squeezed her hand, and she squeezed back. I asked if she needed pain medicine; she shook her head. A Christian station on the radio played this message, the voice in a Texan accent:

T he doctors told her she had cancer. They told her she couldn't be cured. But if she wanted to live a little longer she had to go to a big hospital in Houston.

Well, I tell you, my friends, she got in that car and they started driving to Houston. But she didn't make it to Houston. No, sir. She had a message from God just as clear as if she had a telephone call. She heard this radio station. She heard me talking to folks like I'm talking to you all now. And she knew she could go home.

Because, if you have enough faith in the Lord Jesus, if you turn your heart to him in earnest prayer, you will be healed. Yes, I said, "Will," not might. No maybe about this folks. It's there in the Bible. It's your blessing to be claimed.

She called me up and we started praying. Two months later she went in to see her doctor. Well, you can believe he was mighty surprised to see her. He thought she would be dead by then, I suppose.

"Did you go to Houston?" he said to her.

timid, came and laid his hands on the stroke victim, crying out to God.

Crazy, I thought. Besides, I'd already given the faith healing thing a try.

Then something amazing happened. The man stood from the lawn chair and started walking. He walked fifty feet to the stage and raised his arms in praise and thanksgiving.

Okay. He wasn't completely whole. He limped. But he was carried in, and he walked out.

A couple years later, the pastor who had organized the healing crusade visited the U.S. I asked him about this man with the stroke. He's driving a bus now, he told me.

What happened? Did neurons regenerate and form new synaptic connections? Would a follow-up CT scan post-prayer show resolved stroke areas? Or maybe a simpler explanation: the guy got hope. Instead of accepting his disability, he challenged himself to achieve his ability. But somehow the guy being carried became the guy driving the bus.

What does faith have to do with it?

When Jesus healed the leper, the leper had faith Jesus could do it; he only questioned Jesus's willingness. The centurion's servant may have had no faith in Jesus, but his master did. Peter's mother-in-law may or may not have had faith in Jesus, but Peter certainly did. In a perverse way, even the demons of the Gadarenes had faith in Jesus. And the four guys who brought in the paralyzed man had faith or they wouldn't have gone through the effort. *Someone* had to have faith. Someone had to believe that Jesus was who he said he was, and he had the power to heal.

Faith is not everything needed for healing. God is too smart to do whatever we want him to do even if we believe

—really, truly believe—in him. But faith is an important prerequisite to his intervention. It gets us close enough to touch him.

The unique message about the bleeding woman is this: not only was she healed from her menorrhagia but also was redeemed from her isolation. She had been a pariah, unable to go the synagogue for twelve long years. Under the fear of death, no one had touched her—not her mother, not her father, not her brother or sister, not her closest friend, even if she had one. No one had faith for her. No one brought Jesus to her; no one brought her to Jesus. She was alone when she developed her sneaky plan: *"If only I touch his cloak, I will be healed."*

I have never been this isolated. I have sometimes been lonely in a crowd and sometimes sought solitude in quiet places. But no matter how dark the day, I've always had a mother, father, brother, sister, close friend, child, or, last but not least, my wife to come home to and hug.

I've never suffered anything for twelve years. I have had dark days when I doubted myself, others when outside forces attacked me and looked like they would win, and still others when those I love were sick or dying. Dark days, indeed—but they were days, not years.

I don't know how I'd handle social isolation, weakness, and fatigue for twelve years. I hope to never find out. If it does happen, though, I'm glad to hear that I can elbow my way in through the crowd and grab Jesus by the sleeve, that he will turn around and tell me, *Take heart, my son. Your faith has healed you.*

7

MIRACLE #7

LAUGHING AT THE FUNERAL

While he was saying this, a synagogue leader came and knelt before him and said, "My daughter just died. But come and put your hand on her and she will live." Jesus got up and went with him, and so did his disciples.

Matthew 9:18-19

The patient was nineteen, newly married, and suffered a fatal brainstem hemorrhage while she was sleeping with her new husband. In Jesus's time, she would have simply been dead. But the husband called 911 and began resuscitation. The EMTs took over for the ambulance ride to the hospital, and in the ER she was promptly intubated and placed on a respirator even before the CT scan revealed the cause of her sudden death.

The patient and her family were African American, and I became acutely aware of how white the staff and myself appeared. And though we all spoke English, they spoke in the dialect and syntax of the rural South while I spoke with technical medical terms in the dialect of the urban North. Our very different American experiences met over a bed of tragedy.

Her husband was too young and too traumatized to act as the next-of-kin. Her mother, the person who had known her best, took over the role. I gave the mother the bad news, and she told me they were a praying people, and with all due respect, they would wait and pray. Over the next twenty-four hours the patient fulfilled all the medical and legal criteria—EEG, labs, and repeated exams—for brain death. I talked with the mother again and discussed transplantation donor status or removal from the respirator.

I could feel that her trust in me and my information was reluctant and conditional. Our conversation was marked by a kind of intense cordiality. We didn't look like each other, we didn't sound like each other, but we needed to understand each other. I was disappointed that she wouldn't consider organ donation, but I understood. In the 1980s, racial tensions were more silent but more intense. A few weeks before, facing a similar situation with a white family, they would only agree that the child could be an organ donor if we could guarantee that the organs would not go to a person of color. (We did not guarantee and they did not donate)

The mother asked for another twenty-four hours to give time for her son, a preacher in Georgia, to come and pray for the patient to be raised from the dead. It must have taken courage for her to ask. She must have known I would think the idea ludicrous. I know I had to mask my thoughts with my expression when, knowing I couldn't refuse, I encouraged her and promised to do everything to keep her daughter stable until her son arrived.

I felt very uneasy with the plan. No way would this girl be raised from the brain dead. Their prayers would meet disappointment. Then what? Loss of faith? Blaming the medical profession for the failure? Assigning us the role of the devil?

The next morning the EEG was still flat. The patient's neurological examination remained unchanged. I gave my report to the mother and met the brother, the young preacher from Georgia. While family and friends gathered in the room, I agreed to stay.

"In the name of Jesus, rise and walk!" the brother shouted.

The respirator clunked and wheezed. The heart monitor beeped on. She lay unmoving.

"In the name of Jesus, rise and walk!" he shouted again.

The respirator noises and heart monitor continued to be the only sound.

"In the name of Jesus, rise and walk," he shouted once more.

Nothing changed. After a few minutes I went to the bedside and re-examined the patient. She remained brain dead.

This would be the awkward moment, I thought. They would nod and back off, and leave me to step in as the white man in the white coat who took away their last hope.

But the preacher had one more prayer. "Thank you, Jesus," he said.

Thank you? For what? This was not an answered prayer. The girl remained dead.

"Thank you," he said again. The family members murmured *amens* behind him.

"Thank you," he said, one more time. "We loved our sister, Lord," he said, "but you loved her more. Thank you for her life here with us, and thank you for her eternal life with you."

The family and friends filed by the bedside then, saying their last goodbyes, leaving me alone with the ICU nurse and the brain-dead girl. I turned off the respirator and filled out the death certificate, as I had many times before and would many times again. But this time the sharp line between the living and the dead blurred. Her body had died; her spirit had risen.

W*hen Jesus entered the synagogue leader's house and saw the noisy crowd and people playing pipes, he said, "The girl is not dead but asleep." But they laughed at him. After the crowd had been put outside, he went in and took the girl by the hand, and she got up (Matt. 9: 23-25).*

A man who had just been told to make funeral arrangements for his daughter appeared and knelt before Jesus. He was known as a leader of the synagogue, a preacher maybe. Tears streamed down his cheeks. He had heard about lepers cleansed, fevers cooled, demons banished, and a paralyzed man who walked again. Would it be too much to ask for his little girl to be brought back to life?

Matthew didn't record Jesus's answer. Sometimes he doesn't talk to us; he just gets up and goes with us to the most painful places—this time to a child's deathbed. When Jesus got there, loud wailing and shrill pipes already sounded the beginning of mourning. For the second time that day, he told people they were celebrating the wrong thing.

"The girl is not dead but asleep."

They laughed. I can understand why they didn't believe him, this young guy with a charismatic reputation who hadn't been in the room; what did he know? Death is not a difficult diagnosis—at least it wasn't back then before respirators and criteria for brain death. The transformation from living, even debilitated living, to dead is astonishing, and nothing like going to sleep. Anybody could see she was dead.

Sure, Jesus appeared to be a fool. But laughter, out loud during funeral preparations? I'm always tempted at this point to revise *laughed* into something more understandable, like *scoffed*. But Matthew said *laughed*. Sometimes we laugh when we should cry, and cry when we should laugh.

Matthew doesn't record much detail about what happened after the girl got up. I was praying along with the young preacher from Georgia; never have I wished more to be wrong in my diagnosis. I would have been pretty excited if his sister had arisen. We would have had some kind of celebration! The family, the medical staff, the patient, and me—all colors, all backgrounds—we would have celebrated. We would have laughed. Celebrations don't get any bigger than when mourning turns to dancing.

I expect that the synagogue leader in Jesus's time had a big celebration, a tangible example of what Jesus had been telling people earlier that day: you can't fast at the groom's dinner. When you're with Jesus, you don't experience things the old way—you don't mourn without hope or drink the old wine. You drink new wine from new wineskins. You don't laugh at the same things, and you don't cry at the same things, because all things are new.

Jesus goes with the father who has lost a daughter, and he takes her by the hand. She rises up. Then you can dance. You can celebrate.

You can laugh.

8

MIRACLE #8

THE SECRET OF THE BLIND MEN

As Jesus went on from there, two blind men followed him, calling
out, "Have mercy on us, Son of David!"
When he had gone indoors, the blind men came to him, and he
asked them, "Do you believe that I am able to do this?"
"Yes, Lord," they replied.
Then he touched their eyes and said, "According to your faith let it
be done to you;" and their sight was restored. Jesus warned them
sternly, "See that no one knows about this." But they went out
and spread the news about him all over that region.

Matthew 9:27-31

Soon after I started practice back in the 1980's I
consulted on an elderly woman with neck and arm
pain. The pain was severe enough to keep her in the
hospital for a week on injectable narcotics, but the diagnosis
was uncertain. (This was before MRI scans and CT myelog-
raphy.) Her age and health added significant risk to a

surgical procedure. I advised a wait-and-see plan, knowing most often pains from disk herniations and degenerative changes get better with time.

Unfortunately, she didn't get better. Each day I'd see her and advise patience, and each day she'd tell me to operate. After another week, her internist assured me the surgical risks were not too high and urged me to do something.So, reluctantly, I scheduled an operation that I hoped would work.

On the morning of the surgery, I met with the patient while she was lying on a gurney outside the operating room. I reviewed the procedure and risks, and asked her again if she was sure she wanted to go through with it.

She asked me to lean a little closer. I did. Then she grabbed my necktie and pulled me close, nose to nose. "Listen, Doc," she said, "I want you to fix this thing or not wake me up. Do you understand me now?"

I did understand then, and was sorry I hadn't earlier. She had been chasing after me, begging for mercy. How desperate she had been!

Her surgery went well, and her pain was immediately relieved. Afterward, she didn't say *thank you*. She said *I told you so*.

I had allowed her to beg for mercy because I was uncertain about her pathology and surgical risk. I wonder why Jesus allowed the blind men to beg.

It must have been quite a sight, these two men stumbling along after the crowd, yelling for mercy and using the title "Son of David" as flattery—or maybe as a challenge. Jesus kept going; he'd already had a busy day with John's disciples coming for clarification of holy living, a woman sneaking up on him to heal her bleeding problem, a near funeral where people laughed at him, and a little girl who came back from the dead. Now these two guys, hollering for mercy, wouldn't give up.

Maybe Jesus was just tired. When he raises a little girl from the dead, I think of him as God, and he is. But he also chose the limitations of a human form, and those limitations include physical and emotional exhaustion. Maybe he ignored the blind men because he was too weary to deal with one more problem. He just wanted to go home.

I totally understand. Rest is a precious commodity. Sometimes you can't keep on going. The question becomes not *Do they need help?* but *Can it wait?*

But the blind boys not only followed Jesus home, they followed him inside. Probably Jesus invited them in. He sat them down and asked them if they believed he could do what they wanted.

They had just come from the place where a little girl had been raised from the dead, so, well, yeah. If he could raise the dead, he could heal the blind, right? They called him *Lord* and told him *yes*, and he did the expected: he touched their eyes and their vision returned.

Then he did the unexpected: he warned them not to tell anyone.

He must have known that his stern warning—*See that no one knows about this*—would be an impossible instruction. Imagine years of blindness, then going home with your vision restored:

M om says, more aptly than she realizes, "Oh my God! This is a miracle! What happened?"
"Uhh . . . sorry, Mom. Can't tell you. And, by the way, you remember Joe? The other blind guy I hang with? He can see too."

"What do you mean, you can't tell me? You can't waltz in here like this and keep a secret like that. What have you done? Did you do a deal with the devil?"

"Nothing like that, Mom, really. No deals, no devil. I just can't tell you."

"I changed your swaddling clothes when you were a baby, young man. You will not keep secrets from your mama. If you're not talking, I'm going to see Joe's mom right now. We'll get to the bottom of this."

"Joe can't tell you either, Mom. Come on, please, just let it go."

"This is the biggest thing that's ever happened to me. I'm not letting it go. Wait . . . this doesn't have anything to do with that Jesus guy, the carpenter's son from Nazareth, does it? I heard he was over at the synagogue leader's house today. Some big rigmarole about a sick kid?"

"Can't say, Mom. Anyway, you need anything from the market? Me and Joe are going to go down, hang out, and see if we can get a job."

Mom shakes her head and lets it go for now, but only until he's out of the house. As her son leaves for the market, she heads for Joe's house. His mother knows no more than she does, but neighbors talk.

"Did you hear about the crazy lady, the one who's been bleeding forever, and how she sneaked up and grabbed the hem of Jesus's robe? Some people said she tore off one of the blue tassels, and now she says she stopped bleeding. Then those idiots at the rabbi's house thought his daughter was dead and started the funeral, wailing away until Jesus showed up and threw them out. The girl's fine! Can you imagine? Now they're having a party. Then Jesus heads home, and these two blind guys start following him, hollering for mercy."

"What? Wait. Two blind guys?"

"Oh, I don't know if it was your boy or not. I just heard about it."

"What happened to them?"

"Nothing I guess. Jesus just kept right on walking like he couldn't hear them. Went straight home and went inside."

"And the blind guys?"

The woman shrugs. "Don't rightly know."

Mom is home when her son gets back from the market.

"Good news, Mom. Zebedee is looking for two fishermen to take the place of his boys. You remember James and John? They've left the family business. Simon and Andrew gave up fishing, too, so it could be a great opportunity."

Mom nods. "That is good news, son. By the way, was that you and Joe who were following after the Jesus crowd today, shouting for mercy?"

"Yes."

"So what happened?"

"He went home."

"Then what?"

"Can't say, Mom."

M y mom would have figured it out by now, whether I said anything or not, and I guess that is what happened: *But they went out and spread the news about him all over that region* (Matt. 9: 31). Some secrets are hard to keep. Jesus must have known this, so why did he warn them sternly not to tell?

I don't know.

Maybe he wanted them to know this healing touch was totally personal, not part of a public demonstration of messianic power. Jesus waited until they were inside, then showed them that all they needed was their faith, and not only *could* he heal them, he *would* heal them. He showed them more than power. He showed them love. That's something worth waiting for.

Or maybe he simply wanted to restore their vision. Amazing things were about to happen in Galilee and Samaria and Judah and around the world, and he wanted them to see as well as hear about it.

A few hundred years later, a loudly profane, atheist slave-ship sailor feared for his life during a storm at sea. He called on the Lord to have mercy on him, and his life was spared. He started a new life, eventually learning about Jesus and becoming a small town preacher. A few years later, on New Year's Day, 1773, he wanted to tell the congregation about his spiritual journey, so he wrote a poem. Maybe the words are familiar to you. His name was John Newton, and the poem started like this:

> *Amazing grace! How sweet the sound*
> *That saved a wretch like me!*
> *I once was lost but now am found,*
> *Was blind but now I see.*

Jesus keeps touching eyes, and blind people keep receiving their sight. The blind guys in Capernaum, John Newton, and myself—we don't really need to tell you how it happened. That can remain a secret between Jesus and us. But we want you to know what we saw afterward, when we started to follow him.

9

MIRACLE #9

THE MUTE, THE PRINCE OF DEMONS, AND THE KINGDOM
OF GOD

*While they were going out, a man who was demon-possessed and
could not talk was brought to Jesus.*

Matthew 9:32-34

During my second year of medical school I was
sent with two other students to a community
hospital to learn the fine points of physical examination and bedside manner from an internist who had
been in practice for over twenty years. He greeted us in the
lobby of the hospital and hurried us off to see his new
admission.

Our instructor looked the part. He had immaculately
combed silver hair, a tweed suit with stethoscope ears
protruding from one pocket, a white shirt, and a quiet tie.
His manner was efficient without being quick, his face
serious but friendly. We all wanted to be just like him.

But his eyes gave away something else—anxiety.

As he made our acquaintances, his eyes kept flicking toward the hallway, to the patient rooms. After the short delay for introductions we set off behind him down the hall. He stopped just a few doors later. In the bed by the door lay a late-middle-aged woman, about the same age as our instructor. Her hair was perfect. She even had on makeup, and the sheet was pulled up to her chest then neatly folded down—a picture perfect patient. But even from the foot of the bed, through the eyes of a mere second-year student, it was clear she had suffered a major left hemisphere stroke.

Our instructor examined her quickly and pointed out the drooping lower face that spared the forehead, the right-sided motor deficits that paralyzed the right arm but only weakened the right leg, the "toe sign" on the right that was absent on the left, the left carotid bruit that signaled a narrow artery to the brain, and, in spite of her open eyes and brisk attention to her environment, the complete lack of speech. These were all the signs of a stroke in the distribution of the left middle cerebral artery.

Along with the other students I focused on the patient, busy making a catalog of the physical signs of her stroke and creating a mental image for future reference. I had little experience with real sick people and hungered for as much information as I could glean.

Then I looked from the patient back to the instructor and found him stroking the patient's cheek with the back of his hand. She looked into his eyes, clearly trying to ask something, anxiety just beginning to give way to frustration. His hand slipped down, and he took her paralyzed right hand. He held it a moment, gave her warm smile, nodded, and then left the room. We followed like a pack of puppies.

In the hallway, our distinguished instructor shook his head and seemed near tears. "I have known her for a very long time," he said. Then he proceeded to the nursing station and gave a series of orders, most of which were foreign to us medical students. We marveled at his command of the jargon and his equanimity in what seemed like a very emotional experience.

One of those orders was for inhaled CO_2. The theory back in the sixties and early seventies was that CO_2 would dilate the cerebral arteries and mitigate the effects of the stroke. I understood the theory, but had also seen the latest research that showed the treatment was futile, possibly harmful, because the CO_2 only affected the normal arteries, not the ones in the stroke area. If anything, it shunted blood away from the damage. I didn't say anything; it wasn't my place.

The nurses rushed about to carry out his simple orders, to begin an IV and find a CO_2 tank and nasal cannula. The doctor regained his composure and patiently reviewed the signs and symptoms we had observed. He reviewed the orders he had given the nurses and the reasons for each one. The only one that directly treated the stroke was the CO_2.

Then he looked at us, clearly hoping we knew something more than he did, and asked, "Is there anything else they teach you at the university now on how to treat stroke?"

It was 1973. There was nothing. Aspirin wasn't even on the radar then. The only thing we knew was that CO_2 doesn't work. I didn't want to tell him. I didn't want to take away the one thing he thought he could do. But I did.

We then returned to the bedside. By being a physician dedicated to the latest science, not his habit of practice, he again modeled a good doctor. He went to the CO_2 tank and turned it off, asking the nurse to replace it with oxygen. Then he went to stand at the foot of the bed. He looked at his friend, and she looked back, his sorrow and her fear now unmistakable. He would never hear her speak again.

A stroke like this is caused by a thrombus that blocks the middle cerebral artery. But I think that calling it a demon is not inaccurate.

During the next four years—the last two of medical school, one in surgical internship, and another in neuro-surgery training—I saw many tragedies. In medicine, things don't always happen the way they are supposed to. Results are not predictable or fair. Bad things happen to good people. The converse also seems true—inexplicable good results come to addicts and criminals and just plain unpleasant people who don't bother to take care of them-selves. Medicine is fickle, and life is unfair. But this truth is no less sad, especially for me and the patients I fell in love with. I understood now the grief that came with a silenced voice.

Dr. Joan Venes, our chief of pediatric neurosurgery (and a courageous pioneer for women in neurosurgery), called me to her clinic when I was a first-year resident. She intro-duced me to a new patient, Sam. He was nine-years-old, a pudgy, round-faced, happy, sweet kid. He had complained of headaches, severe enough and frequent enough that they earned him a CT scan. With further questioning, I discov-ered that Sam was an average student, not much of an athlete, and dearly loved by his mom and classmates.

The CT scan showed quite dramatic hydrocephalus, a buildup of cerebrospinal fluid (CSF) in the central cavities (ventricles) of the brain. This is not an unusual problem in children, but usually is diagnosed in infancy. To treat his headaches and preserve his future intellectual development, Dr. Venes recommended a shunt procedure to drain the excess CSF into another body cavity where it would be rapidly absorbed back into the bloodstream. I helped her do the surgery. Sam went home five days later, and we felt good about his future.

A few days later Sam came back with worse headaches. A CT scan showed his hydrocephalus had been over treated. The CSF-containing ventricles had shrunken in size and the brain had expanded, but the pressure change in the middle of the brain had occurred too rapidly. The surface of the brain had collapsed away from the inner skull causing bleeding, a condition known as subdural hematoma.

Dr. Venes and I took Sam back to surgery, drained the subdural hematoma, and removed the shunt, leaving an external CSF drain that we could open and close at the bedside if the pressure in his head became either too high or too low. Unfortunately, after the surgery, Sam woke in a bizarre kind of coma, twitching and groaning, unable to even open his eyes. He had unexplained fevers alternating with hypothermia. We attributed his state to "torsion on the brainstem" and his twitching to "thalamic fits," but we really didn't know what had happened.

For the next three weeks he stayed in the ICU while we regulated the pressure in his head and supported his breathing. Many complications plagued Sam, seemingly something new each day, including an infection in the drainage tube. When the pressure stabilized and CT scans showed complete resolution of the subdural hematoma, we took him back to surgery and placed a new shunt with a higher-pressure valve.

After this operation, Sam improved from coma to a

neuro-vegetative state. He opened his eyes and breathed normally, but never moved or spoke. For ten days straight, I came to his bedside, now out of the ICU, and did a sterile tap of the reservoir to sample the fluid and inject an antibiotic. His mother was always there. I would talk to Sam as if he understood, explain to him what I was doing and why, tell him about the weather and baseball scores. He simply stared straight ahead. After a few days, he would move and even chew and swallow if someone fed him. But he still didn't fix his gaze on anyone or speak.

Finally, the CSF samples showed no sign of infection, and the CT scans showed treated hydrocephalus with no subdural hematoma. We had done all we knew how to do. He could go home, a silent child in a wheelchair.

I came by one more time to remove all the bandages and check all the wounds. As usual, I kept up my banter about bandages and baseball, and then stood silently at the end of his bed. I felt guilty about taking a happy kid with a headache and turning him into a nursing home patient while traveling the "road of good intentions." I was angry with my chosen profession. Mentally, I was begging forgiveness and saying good-bye.

Then he fixed his eyes on mine and, with great effort, said, "Thank you, Dr. Lohse."

I was astounded. After seeing so many tragedies, the sound of a lost voice seemed unbelievable.

A*nd when the demon had been driven out, the man who had been mute spoke. The crowd was amazed and said, "Nothing like this has been seen in Israel."*
But the Pharisees said, "It is by the prince of demons that he drives out demons." (Matt. 9: 32-34)

. . .

J esus had just finished healing the blind boys and swearing them to secrecy (which, of course, they didn't do.) Next, he left his home with his friends and was accosted by someone with a man who could not talk. This time the demon was driven out, but Jesus didn't bother to ask them to keep it quiet. Maybe he gave up on secrecy. Or maybe he wanted the Pharisees to hear about it.

When Sam started talking, I was amazed and delighted. Dr. Venes was, too. But nobody else seemed to think much about it. *Yes, yes*, other residents would say, *he finally recovered. Functioning shunt, no infection—the brain recovers nicely sometimes due to resilient neurochemistry that we don't really understand.*

Matthew didn't record a response from Jesus to the Pharisees this time. But, a few chapters later, in Matthew 12:22-23, Jesus heals a man both deaf and mute, and the Pharisees, apparently encouraged by Jesus's previous silence on the point, repeat their accusation: *"It is only by Beelzebub, the prince of demons, that this fellow drives out demons."*

This time, Jesus answers his critics. *"Every kingdom divided against itself will be ruined . . . If Satan drives out Satan, how can his kingdom stand? . . . But if it is by the Spirit of God that I drive out demons, then the Kingdom of God has come upon you."* (Matt. 12:25-28)

I don't talk much about demons and the prince of demons. I understand events in the physical realm in terms of cause and effect. But sometimes something good happens that is so prayed for, and so unlikely, that the term *miracle* can be used. If I speculate about pseudo-scientific causes to explain those miracles, then maybe that talk is the 21st

century version of demons and the prince of demons. Instead I should choose to think that when Sam says *thank you,* a lost voice speaks, and the Kingdom of God has come upon me.

10

MIRACLE #10
SHRIVELED HAND AND SHRIVELED HEART

Going on from that place, he went into their synagogue, and a man with a shriveled hand was there. Looking for a reason to bring charges against Jesus, they asked him, "Is it lawful to heal on the Sabbath?"

Matthew 12: 9-10

The blood bank had some rules about withdrawals in the 1970s, bad rules. Only interns or residents could sign out blood, and they could take only one unit at a time. With this system, the leadership felt confident that the right patient would likely get the right unit of blood, the numbers on the units would be carefully checked, and the blood supply would be used safely and carefully. A valuable resource would not be wasted. The blood bank director and staff cared about patient safety to the extent that they were passionate about preventing transfusion reactions.

This sounds good, but it is not. They had forgotten the reason the blood bank existed.

They saw only refrigerated blood in plastic containers. They never felt hot blood from an arterial bleeder hit them in the face, never saw blood running out of open wounds, drenching bandages, soaking sheets, or dripping onto the floor, and they never mopped up afterward. They had forgotten that they existed to get blood into the veins of the critically ill who would otherwise be dead.

One day a man came into the ER after a gunshot wound to the upper right chest. Already unconscious, his blood pressure read dangerously low, varying between shock and simply undetectable. Large volumes of fluid were pumped into newly started IV lines, and a tube was placed into his airway to assure oxygenation of the small amount of still circulating blood. Also, a chest tube was placed to allow expansion of the lung.

The bleeding and consequent hemodynamic shock continued. A cloud of death hovered over the resuscitation. Hopelessness crept closer.

Then the chief resident of cardio-thoracic surgery, a 31-year-old seasoned veteran of the hospital training program, showed up and took charge. He slashed open the entrance wound, inserted his hand, and grabbed the right subclavian artery, his fingertips squeezing it a very few inches from the heart. He called for someone to tell the Operating Room that he was on his way, and, if they didn't have a room open, to get the necessary instruments and personnel into the hallway, and he would start there.

A glimmer of hope came back to the trauma room.

Then he turned to the intern, one of my classmates, and said, "Go to the blood bank and get six units of O-negative blood."

O-negative is the blood type least likely to cause a reaction if given to a patient of unknown blood type. It is transfused without typing the patient's blood and specifically cross matching it only in circumstances like this, when time is critical.

To do what the chief resident requested the intern to do would break the blood bank rules. He started to object, "But—"

"Just get the blood and meet me in the operating room," the chief said. He knew this patient's survival depended on not only skill and luck, but on this intern's willingness to break the rules.

The elevators were slow and unreliable, so the intern ran the six flights of stairs up to the blood bank. He arrived out of breath and told the medical technologist what he needed. She said she would work on the cross-match as soon as she received a sample from the patient, and the first unit should be ready in fifteen minutes.

"You don't understand," the intern said.

"We've got rules," she replied. "And if I break them, I get fired. If you break them, you get fired."

The intern didn't say another word. He went to the storage refrigerator, took six units of O-negative blood and went to the operating room.

The patient survived.

The intern didn't get fired. Neither did he get commended. He got a reprimand and a warning, because it was only his first offense.

Jesus was working on his second offense of the day. He had just had a run-in with the religious right after his followers ate a few kernels of grain while walking through a field on the Sabbath, breaking the Fourth Commandment. This time, Jesus didn't remain silent. He told them to learn what God meant when he had told the prophet Hosea, "I desire mercy, not sacrifice."

The rule experts didn't answer, but they simmered with resentment.

After the confrontation in the field, Jesus, his followers, and these same religious rule experts walked into town. They went to the synagogue and found a man with a shriveled hand.

Knowing about Jesus's reputation for healing, the rule experts jumped on the opportunity. In the field, only the followers were accused of breaking the Sabbath. Here, Jesus himself would be tempted to do the same.

"Is it lawful to heal on the Sabbath?" they asked him.

In other words, *Aren't you supposed to be resting? It's not an emergency. What's the guy even supposed to do with a healed hand on the Sabbath? Nothing: he's supposed to be resting, too.*

Jesus answers. "If any of you has a sheep and it falls into a pit on the Sabbath, will you not take hold of it and lift it out? How much more valuable is a person than a sheep! Therefore it is lawful to do good on the Sabbath."

They must have had a soft spot for their sheep, because nobody said a word. The man stretched out his hand, and it became good as new. This should have been the happy ending of the story.

But it wasn't. The rule experts left the synagogue and started planning a murder.

Jesus didn't generally advocate breaking the law, but he gave us a lesson about rules. Don't miss an opportunity to be merciful. God desires mercy.

The Pharisees missed the point of the lesson about the kernels of grain. They missed it again about the shriveled hand. And it is a dangerous lesson to miss, because it's a terrible thing to fall in love with the rulebook. You forget who God is, and what he expects. You forget you exist out of his mercy, and are created to show mercy. Your heart shrivels. Someone could bleed to death.

11

MIRACLE # 11

DEMONS AND HUNGRY DOGS

Leaving that place, Jesus withdrew to the region of Tyre and Sidon. A Canaanite woman from that vicinity came to him, crying out, "Lord, Son of David, have mercy on me! My daughter is demon-possessed and suffering terribly."

Matthew 15:21-22

In 2003, in a roadless village on a muddy Central American riverbank, a mother brought her nine-year-old daughter to our makeshift, one-day mission clinic. She had a similar story to the Canaanite woman's, the mother who pestered Jesus.

The house where we held the clinic sat on a mud embankment a dozen feet above a dock at the edge of a fast-flowing stream. Electricity and indoor plumbing had yet to reach this small community, but the house had a solid concrete foundation, a good roof, and generous windows for circulation and light. Air hung damp and heavy with the barest breeze, a vague suggestion that rain would bring relief from the heat. But the rain never came, and the house became hotter and hotter under the afternoon sun.

Two college kids served as my assistants. One translated Spanish, and the other served as my pharmacist. That morning, we had been dropped off at this house by a motorized dugout canoe and promised an afternoon pick-up that would get us back to the mission base camp before dark.

The patients had the common ailments: parasites, water-borne illnesses, fatigue, and pain. We carried with us the common temporary fixes: anti-parasitics, antibiotics, adult vitamins with iron, children's vitamins without, and many bottles of ibuprofen and acetaminophen. I freely dispensed advice about water purification, hand washing, and sleeping off the ground to prevent parasites—advice soundly based in the principles of medicine and regularly ignored in the reality of tropical subsistence farming, hunting-gathering, and irregular migrant labor work. Our goals were modest: temporary relief of pain and suffering, a blip of preventative health measures, and a witness to the love of Jesus.

By mid-afternoon the heat and humidity weighed on me like a damp, wool blanket. My butt ached from sitting, my joints stiffened, and a weariness crawled over whatever good intentions I had started with. After a few days in a country where almost no one spoke English, the feeling of alienation was inevitable—the literal experience of being a stranger in a strange land. I began to wonder why I was there. This is what a crisis of faith feels like. I looked at my watch and wished the boat to come soon.

Then our last patient came, a nine-year-old girl accompanied by her mother. Like many people in that area, they were refugees from the violence of the socialist regime in the nation across the river. The mother demanded to know what was wrong with her child.

I looked her over and found nothing wrong. If anything, the child was better nourished, with less evidence of parasites than the other children I had seen that day. I told the mother my opinion.

"But there is something wrong with her," she said. "She cannot do her schoolwork. Two or three times each week her body stiffens, and she falls to the ground and urinates on herself. Then she must come home. Other times, several times each day, she stares off in space without speaking. No one can talk to her for a minute, or two, or three. Then she will be confused and know nothing. The teachers tell me to stop bringing her to school because she cannot learn."

The diagnosis became clear to me. The girl had a seizure disorder, generalized, or *gran mal*, episodes with frequent minor seizures, absence spells. A variety of anticonvulsant medications exist that can control these symptoms in the great majority of cases. But I had none of these with me, nor would I be able to do the long-term monitoring and medication changes that would optimize her care.

I explained to the mother what I felt certain was the problem, and suggested we make a referral to a doctor at a town a few miles up the river. Then the mother explained to me that she had already been there, and even taken her daughter to a public health clinic in the capital city. No one believed her story; no more tests had been performed and no medicines prescribed, perhaps because she was an illegal alien.

Other times when I had worked in this country, I had local medical contacts where I could make referrals. But this was the first time I had been in this province and, at the moment, I had no solution. I hoped that Anna, the permanent missionary in the area, would know the necessary local medical network well enough to make the right referral.

Just then I heard the puttering of an outboard motor. Our canoe had come. It was time to pack up and go home. I looked out the glassless window to see Anna in the over-sized canoe approach the dock.

Anna was middle-aged, strong and stout, and outspoken to the point of being rude, seemingly an odd choice for Jesus's local representative. She lacked the gentle demeanor usually associated with the Savior. But she did have his courage, and his heart for the poor and the lost.

Anna marched from the dock to the house and demanded to know if we were ready to go. I told her my frustration with my last patient. "We've got nothing to offer her," I said.

"Nothing to offer?" she spouted. "Of course we have something to offer. Where is that little girl?"

When I indicated the girl and her mother, Anna grabbed my arm and pulled me toward them. I thought she had some additional medical resources or knew where to refer the child. Instead, she spoke a few words in Spanish, and then put her hand and mine on the girl's head. She bowed her head, spoke in a torrent of Spanish and added a brief prayer in English for my benefit. "In the Name of Jesus, be healed!"

Then she said a few gentle words to the mother before stomping away while muttering something like, "Nothing to offer, indeed." She bullied us all, along with our supplies, into the canoe, now muttering "Time's a-wasting," and "You don't want to be on this river after dark." In a few minutes we puttered away.

I'd like to report that my patient was "healed from that moment." But did the little refugee girl in Central America have continued seizures, or was she miraculously healed? Or did she finally find a sympathetic and skilled doctor, and respond well to medical treatment? I don't know. I can only hope.

L eaving that place, Jesus withdrew to the region of Tyre and Sidon. A Canaanite woman from that vicinity came to him, crying out, "Lord, Son of David, have mercy on me! My daughter is demon-possessed and suffering terribly."

Jesus did not answer a word. So his disciples came to him and urged him, "Send her away, for she keeps crying out after us."

He answered, "I was sent only to the lost sheep of Israel."

The woman came and knelt before him. "Lord, help me!" she said.

He replied, "It is not right to take the children's bread and toss it to the dogs."

"Yes it is, Lord," she said. "Even the dogs eat the crumbs that fall from their master's table."

Then Jesus said to her, "Woman, you have great faith! Your request is granted." And her daughter was healed at that moment (Matt. 15:21-28).

T he religious leaders of Jesus's home country plotted to kill him. His family thought he had lost his mind and tried to interrupt his preaching. His hometown shunned him. And his cousin, friend, and partner in ministry, John the Baptist, had just been executed. Yet crowds pressed on him wherever he went. Everybody wanted something. Some wanted to be healed; some wanted him to be quiet; some wanted him dead.

The demands of the crowd and the persecution from those in power drove him out of the country. He retreated to the coastal plain in what is now Lebanon, where he would be relatively unknown. Remember when the devil tempted Jesus in the wilderness? *When the devil finished all this tempting, he left him until a more opportune time* (Luke 4:13). Maybe this was "the more opportune time," and maybe the doubt sown by the devil was for Jesus to wonder if he had really heard the voice of his Father and, if so, why was it so hard?

Jesus wasn't the first to be thrown into doubt and chased from his mission. Moses fled to Midian, David to the wilderness of Judea, and Elijah to Mount Horeb—all of them experiencing early strength and success before falling into fear and uncertainty. They all retreated. Jesus, like the other great leaders, had good reason to flee the country and seek peace.

But peace eluded him. A Canaanite woman, a descendant of the people Israel displaced when they took over the Promised Land, pestered him to drive out a demon. She had the tenacity of a mother with a sick child.

"Demon possession" implies mental illness or epilepsy, the likely diagnosis for this Canaanite. The ancient Greeks called epilepsy *The Sacred Disease.* Hippocrates wrote an essay about it 400 years before Jesus was born. The mother's perseverance is totally understandable. There were no cures.

But Jesus, already forced to be a stranger in a strange land, and now beset by a woman in the tribe of his people's ancient enemy, didn't say a word. He didn't agree to heal the girl, but much to his disciples' dismay, he wouldn't send her away either. You can hear the disciples saying, "Not our problem," and turning to Jesus for confirmation.

Understanding Jesus in his human form is so much

more difficult than understanding him as God incarnate. Because as God incarnate, he already has the right answers and already knows the future. But the little windows we have into his humanity—his hesitancy to solve the wine problem at the wedding, his temptation in the wilderness, his prayer in the Garden of Gethsemane—all tell us that he *didn't* have all the answers. But he did have that peculiar faith that listens to the Father's voice even when the Father hasn't been saying much recently.

Jesus had been trying to keep a low profile, hoarding his energy and restoring his sense of direction. I don't know what it cost him personally to heal somebody, but my experience with life and the principles of economics and physics tells me that nothing is free. Each healing experience cost Jesus something we don't understand. He needed a little space, and now this woman kneeled in that space. He could not avoid her.

God sent Moses a burning bush; he sent David an army and Elijah a "still, small voice."

Then God the Father sent Jesus a messenger in the form of a desperate mother, someone who needed him and had faith in him, to beg him to bring hope to a hopeless child. *Take one more step*, the Father said. *Even if it is beyond what you thought your ministry was about, even if it is out of your comfort zone.*

To our eternal benefit, Jesus took one more step, healing a strange girl in a strange land from a strange illness. Then he took another step, and another. In a few days he had returned to the shores of the Sea of Galilee: *Great crowds came to him, bringing the lame, the blind, the crippled, the mute and many others, and laid them at his feet; and he healed them* (Matt. 15:29).

Sometimes I feel that in spite of my obedience to the

Father's voice, I experience nothing but criticism, that whatever I do is no more than feeding crumbs to the dogs. Then God sends someone who needs Jesus, like the little girl with the seizure disorder, and someone, like Anna, who guides me, and I take one more step.

12

MIRACLE #12

MOUNTAINS AND MUSTARD SEEDS

When they came to the crowd, a man approached Jesus and knelt
before him. "Lord, have mercy on my son," he said. "He has
seizures and is suffering greatly. He often falls into the fire or into
the water. I brought him to your disciples, but they could not heal
him."

Matthew 17:14-16

Our internship class inherited a man named Archibald, or "Archie" as everyone quickly came to know him. About a week before our internship started, he had suffered a shotgun wound to the abdomen when a heroin deal went south and had his first of many operations to save his life. Any abdominal wound can be fatal, but a shotgun is particularly nasty because of the multiple intestinal perforations, each of which can be the source of infection—peritonitis—and potentially life-threatening sepsis. Some of the intestine can be sacrificed, but if too much intestine is taken, the body cannot absorb adequate nutrition to survive.

Archie survived his first operation but had recurring bouts of peritonitis and sepsis. At one point his respiration failed, and he needed a ventilator for nearly a month. To "rest" his intestine and minimize further infection he required total parenteral nutrition, TPN, through central intravenous lines. Over the next few months, he underwent several more operations to find and repair damaged intestines or drain abscesses. Every surgical intern who rotated through general surgery took care of Archie.

He was a likable guy. We—all eighteen interns— suffered with him and never lost hope for his eventual healing, even though each week seemed to bring a new complication. The months dragged on; through all of them, no friends or family members visited. We had the feeling that he had become part of our family at the hospital—the pseudo-family that comes together when dedicated people work in unity for a common cause.

Finally, one day in early spring, word spread to the interns scattered throughout the hospital: after nine months, Archie had made it out of the ICU! A few days later —miracle of miracles—he was released from the hospital. The interns and ICU nurses actually had a party for him. With cake!

But three days later, he was back in the ER with a new abdominal problem. This time he had been stabbed. He actually looked sheepish. He knew how much literal blood, sweat, and tears had poured into his care. Then we did what we do; we took care of him again. But we were deeply disappointed.

At least the care was simpler this time. Knife wounds are ever so much easier than shotgun wounds. A few weeks later, Archie was discharged once more, and we never saw him again. Maybe he mended his ways. Or maybe he moved, or maybe he died after the next injury. I don't know.

What I know is the change that happened in us, his care-givers. We lost a certain enthusiasm for our unbridled altru-ism, recognizing that sometimes we care more and work harder at fixing our patient's injuries than they work at saving their own lives.

Or that's the way it seems. Another way of saying this is that we could fix complicated abdominal injuries, but we couldn't fix addictions, broken neighborhoods, and dysfunc-tional relationships— and if those things did not get fixed, all our other efforts were in vain.

W*hen they came to the crowd, a man approached Jesus and knelt before him. "Lord, have mercy on my son," he said. "He has seizures and is suffering greatly. He often falls into the fire or into the water. I brought him to your disciples, but they could not heal him."*

"You unbelieving and perverse generation," Jesus replied, "how long shall I stay with you? How long shall I put up with you? Bring the boy here to me." Jesus rebuked the demon and it came out of the boy, and he was healed at that moment (Matt. 17:14-18).

J esus had been coy with patients before, taking his time before responding to their requests, calling them out when they touched his robe, forgiving sins instead of commanding healing, casting out demons from the violent men of the Gadarenes without being asked—all unexpected responses to human suffering. But never had he been impatient, even rude, as he was now to a father with an epileptic son.

Or maybe his comments about the "unbelieving and perverse generation" had been directed elsewhere—maybe to the disciples, because of their failure to cure the child in his absence. But even this seems unfair and out of character for the Jesus we have come to know in the previous chapters. Or maybe he's human—not *just* human, but still *human,* like you and me.

He had just come down from the mountain. He had been in the presence of Moses and Elijah, the great leaders and prophets, both of whom the world believed long dead. And God himself spoke to them and Jesus in the presence of three witnesses: *This is my Son, whom I love; with him I am well pleased. Listen to him* (Matt. 17:5)!

How many of us wouldn't love to hear those same words from our earthly fathers! Or if we have been lucky enough to hear them, don't we treasure those moments among the best in our lives? Imagine hearing the clear voice of God the Father while communing with the saints of the past. This had to be the pinnacle of his life on earth so far—what he had meant when he talked about "The Kingdom of God," a place he knew in faith and in hope but had yet to experience in earthly life.

Then he came down from the mountain and found the same kind of problems he had left the day before, along with disciples who couldn't seem to make any headway without his presence. No doubt the disciples looked sheepish. After Jesus had his little outburst, he did what Jesus does; he cast out the demon.

"How long shall I stay with you?" he cried out, but maybe

he was really questioning his Father whom he had just left: *How long until I can come home? How long until every soul has unity with you? How long will our created world be filled with diseases and demons?*

Maybe what we felt when Archie came back to the ER with his stab wound is something like what Jesus felt. Every effort falls short unless "the Kingdom comes."

T*hen the disciples came to Jesus in private and asked, "Why couldn't we drive it out?"*

He replied, "Because you have so little faith. Truly I tell you, if you have faith as small as a mustard seed, you can say to this mountain, 'Move from here to there,' and it will move. Nothing will be impossible for you." (Matt. 17:19-20)

J esus had previously commissioned the disciples to "heal the sick, raise the dead, cleanse those who have leprosy, drive out demons" (Matt. 10:5), and they had been successful. But not this time. When Jesus returned and dealt with the problem they couldn't solve, they couldn't understand their failure. They had to know.

Up to this point, the disciples had been successful in facing problems similar to the boy with the seizure disorder. And they had given up their jobs and homes to follow Jesus. Already they had risked their livelihoods and very lives. How could Jesus tell them that they had so little faith? What could more faith look like?

I don't know. But the mountain Jesus talked about was the mountain he had just come from—the Kingdom of God experience of being united with our Father and the saints. If you have faith like a mustard seed, you can move this mountain of misery and the Kingdom comes.

One of the most common spinal conditions I cared for was a herniated lumbar disc. The results in a typical case were gratifying—90% of patients felt improved and returned to normal activities. 5% took a little longer and maybe a second operation. But another 5% never got better, descending into a nightmare of chronic pain and disability, and the reasons for failure were often obscure. Sometimes I felt the failures were my own—misdiagnosis, clumsy handling of the delicate nerve, failure to remove enough of the disc, or even removing too much disk or too much bone during the exposure. More often, I could find no difference between an operation I had done on a successful case and an operation on a failed case. Nevertheless, every failure was personal. I wanted desperately to know why this time I couldn't drive out the demons of pain and disability.

One of the most difficult things for a surgeon to do after a failure is to see the next patient. When I walk from one patient still in pain weeks after what should have been a successful operation and go to another still in pain after weeks of non-operative treatment for the same condition, it's hard to turn the doorknob. I know what is most likely to give the second patient relief, and I know it is an operation that I am trained to do as well as anyone in the world. I know what this patient wants and what medical science recommends and what I am going to say. But it's hard. Because after the doorknob is turned, and I step into the room, everything else will happen, and the results will be on me. At those moments I have little faith, no bigger than a mustard seed, and I don't want to do it.

Then I turn the knob, take a step into the room, hold out my hand to theirs, and listen. We do the examination and look at the images, and together we work out a plan. And, most of the time, the mountain of pain and disability moves from here to there. Then, to one more little corner of creation, the Kingdom comes.

13

MIRACLE #13
TWO BLIND PEOPLE

As Jesus and his disciples were leaving Jericho, a large crowd
followed him. Two blind men were sitting by the roadside, and
when they heard that Jesus was passing by, they shouted, "Lord,
Son of David, have mercy on us!"

Matthew 20:29-31

E vil Incarnate—those were the words that came
into my mind as I looked at the MRI image of a
giant tumor, its irregular borders and varying
densities spreading near the geometric center of the brain.
The natural history of this tumor would be progressive
disability, loss of intellect, coma, and death within a few
weeks.

Evil Incarnate is a pineal area tumor. The most common
variation in a patient like this teen-age boy would be a
germinoma, something familiar to me. Treatment plans
were nearly as varied as the number of neurosurgical

centers, since at that time the long-term outcome studies for the various treatments had not established the best therapy. Outcome was guarded, depending not only on treatment plan, but also on the pathology of the tumor cells, which could only be determined by biopsy and spinal fluid analysis.

But germinoma was not the first word that came to my mind.

Because this time the MRI image was of Adam, my handsome 16-year-old son with the blond crew cut, the gymnast's body, and the poet's heart.

Evil Incarnate.

The words had been forming for the previous five months for another reason. My wife, Mary, and I were still dealing with the aftermath of the abnormal mammogram, the needle biopsy that diagnosed cancer, the bilateral mastectomy, and the subsequent chemotherapy every two weeks. At the time of our son's MRI, there was still more chemotherapy scheduled for Mary.

Oh yes, she had a good prognosis, but the estimated 90% five-year survival for this size and type of tumor sounded so much better when it was about someone else. Ninety percent survival feels so good to say when it rolls off our tongue as doctors; we've all had to say much worse. But, as the patient's husband, my first thought was, *that's not good enough.* I did not want to see my wife with a 10% mortality over the next five years. She would have been safer on the front lines in Vietnam. And what about the next five years, and the five after that?

No, cancer with a good prognosis is still not good. It is better than cancer with a bad prognosis, but it is not life simply going forward. It is facing mortality. It is Mary bargaining with life and death: *I'll trade the violence of surgery and the poison of chemotherapy for more days in this time-space continuum on this planet. I'll do it for the sake of those I love and who love me—for my children and husband—so that they will not miss me when I am gone, at least not for a long time. By then they will be older, and it won't be so painful. And I know this pain from my father's death when I was 12, and how I learned that, heaven or no heaven, dead is dead. He was not there and is not here, and I do not wish my children to know what it is like to have a parent die while they are still children. So bring it on. Bring on the scalpel and the scars; good-bye to those symbols of my sexuality. Bring on the drugs and the nausea and the hair loss. I will do what I need to do to fight for life, because I am not fighting only for my life; I am fighting for my children.*

Mary and I hung onto the teddy bear called Good Prognosis, pushing down our fears, re-assuring our children. We fought for normality, pretending that life simply went on, and we were doing a pretty good job of it. Then I saw Evil Incarnate.

Looking at that image, I wished for the first time that I was not a neurosurgeon. I wished that I did not know what that image represented. I wished that I did not know what pain surgery caused. I wished that I did not know the risks: visual loss, intellectual impairment, paralysis. I wished that I did not know what it looked like to die from pineal tumors. And most of all, at that moment, I wished that I did not have to be the one to tell my son and my wife.

The next week, Adam had surgery. The following week, Mary had her last chemotherapy. The subsequent week, Adam started radiation therapy. The next month Adam started having pain in his abdomen. The following month he had another operation to remove an infected shunt. Each day his temperature would spike to 104 ^{0} F, and twice daily a nurse would come to the house to administer IV antibiotics. I thought he would die.

Then, the bad year was over. By January we were done with treatments. Mary and Adam started recovering physically, but had been left with hard consequences. Mary had lost her figure, and Adam had gone from being a gymnast to a kid who couldn't jump high enough to get his feet off the ground.

But we were okay. We had a Good Prognosis. We were healing. We would get better. We went to school; we went to work. We went to church. We ate and slept, read books, went to movies and had birthday parties. Life would go on. We were sure of it.

Or at least this is what I said. I was the cheerleader. When Mary or Adam expressed their sense of loss or concern for the future, I would grab the Good Prognosis teddy bear and wave him in front of them, pet him, and hold him up high. I would say, *Everything will be okay*.

But everything was not okay. Mary and Adam both experienced a profound sense of loss from who they had been to who they were now. Double vision never left Adam, painful scars never left Mary, and the scars were more than skin deep. We had a new household resident named Fear. Because from that time forward, a cough was not a cough; it was metastatic cancer. A headache was not a headache; it was a recurrent brain tumor. Weariness or nausea brought the *deja vu* of chemotherapy.

Time does not heal all wounds, but at least it allows the detritus of life to cover the scars and make some bad things easier to forget. Fears without foundation became more rare. A cough became just a cough, a cold became a cold, a headache became a headache; double vision was just something that happened when one got tired. The pain in Mary's scars eventually faded, and she got clothes to accommodate her new figure. Adam's hair grew back, and although he was never again a gymnast, he could hike the Appalachian Trail and play chess and go to college. If we learned any one truth about the purpose of life it was that the most important thing was to love each other, and be loved. For without that, our lives were not worth the battles it took to live them.

In spite of that, we each drifted down into the darkness of our own deep depression. With the resilience of youth, Adam may have felt it less acutely, but Mary had periods of tears, self-imposed social isolation, feelings of hopelessness, and an inability to plan for the future. Waving my teddy bear didn't help. Here is her story in her own words:

O*ur "bad year," 1991, ended in December with Adam having yet another brain surgery to remove an infected shunt, and my chemotherapy sessions completed. As we moved into a new season and a new year, Adam went back to school, weak and bald, skinny and scarred, but a survivor, completing his junior year in high school. I was depressed.*

All the adrenalin that had kept me going for eight months left. I had gained forty pounds during that season and I was embarrassed about my appearance, which had more to do with being fat than mastectomy scars. I was ashamed that instead of praising God with great joy for the healing taking place in Adam and me, I felt only a sad disappointment that we had gone through all of the pain, the fear, the scars for who-knew-why. I was disillusioned to say the least. As my depression grew, I felt everyone watching me and judging me, wondering if my faith was firm; wondering why this had happened to us; wondering if we were worthy of all the prayers and casseroles and help that had been heaped on us by loving friends and family.

As we moved into spring, it became harder and harder to leave the house and face the outside world. Dean took the children to church alone, week after week, while I stayed home and grieved. My sadness had become commonplace in our home.

Palm Sunday has always been special to us because our daughter, Brieanna, was born on Palm Sunday in 1983. I had looked forward to that service every year. But not this year. I dressed the children, sent them off with their dad and went to the kitchen with tears, which had become commonplace, rolling down my cheeks. I wish I could go to church with my family, I wept. And then, I "heard" a quiet, firm voice ask deep in my soul, Why don't you?

I don't think this was an auditory voice, but it was as real as if someone stood right behind me. I answered the Lord of the Universe (for I knew it was him), I don't have anything to wear that fits, and I heard nothing for a moment as I cried even harder. Then he said, Mary, you can't help how you feel, but you can choose what you do.

I knew in my heart that this was a watershed moment. I didn't dare stay home. With fear and trembling, I found something to wear, got in the car, and drove to church.

We worshipped in a traditional, conservative and beautiful church at that time. People noticed what you wore, and coming in late was frowned upon. I knew I would be noticed because not only was I late, but also I hadn't been to church in some time. I parked my car in the one remaining parking spot out front but was unable to get out of the car. Lord, I don't want to walk into that church by myself, I said.

You won't be alone, I heard God reply. I didn't want to be rude, and I knew God had promised to never leave us and that he was always by my side, but that really wasn't what I was talking about. I wanted the physical presence of love that could be touched and smelled and seen. But I got out of the car and started down the sidewalk.

Meanwhile, my husband, with our three children, was singing the opening hymn when he was called out to the foyer. A deacon explained that there had been a car accident and that he was needed. Dean's first thought was that I had been injured somehow. He'd had difficulty leaving me alone when I was so distressed that morning, and he was frightened. "Is it Mary?" he asked. He was told that it had to do with his car instead and he was puzzled. His car was safely parked outside the church.

He went outside to find a sweet little old lady saying that she was so sorry she'd run into his parked car. She kept saying that she didn't know what happened. Her car apparently had a mind of its own, for it plowed right into Dean's BMW as she was driving past the church. It was just a little fender bender, Dean assured her, and he moved back to the sidewalk just in time to meet me, walking slowly toward the church. He gave me a huge hug as I asked him what he was doing outside. He said, "I thought I was checking on my car, but I guess I was coming out to take my wife to church." We walked in together and the children snuggled close and the sun shone through tall windows, and the choir sang and my tears dried. My depression was over.

As Mary recovered from her depression, Adam resumed the trajectory of his life, and we all returned to something like normal, I drifted into my own depression.

I had always been a fix-it guy. Why else go into medicine and surgery? Fix the problem, save lives, alleviate pain and suffering, prevent disability—that was what it was all about. But now I had just learned that all fixes were temporary, and

I could not shake off the implications: we have no control, death is inevitable, we are dust, and my accomplishments are trivial.

I survived by working, but now I never had the illusion that on a good day I saved a life; the best I could ever do was to prolong one. I distracted myself by learning to draw, trying to play the saxophone, and playing golf. I learned to be a better listener to my wife and children, and to be around more, to be a better dad. I would like to think that I was a more compassionate physician with a deeper understanding of my patients' suffering.

But my heart was heavy, and I simply waited for the next day of darkness.

One spring, on a Good Friday, I got home from work by mid-afternoon. No one else was home, and I went into our back yard to do nothing but feel blue. I reflected on the fact that it was the day that even Christians celebrated death. I tried to think of the things that everyone knows for sure, the things *I* could know for sure. There must be solid ground. Of what could I be certain?

Death and taxes, of course, but the inclusion of taxes is more a matter of humor than philosophy. Death then, for sure. And time, space, matter, and energy. But time ticks on without any end in sight. Space is infinite. Energy is simply another form of matter, and matter is mysterious, understood only by mathematical models that give us illusions, sometimes of charged particles, sometimes of energy packets, or sometimes of more bizarre forms predicted by quantum physics. And now we know that even for any particle to be defined in our universe it must pass through the Higgs field to become real.

In other words, we live for a short time in a universe

without understanding of our basic make-up or destiny. We are dust.

Then I remembered a book title, *Your God is Too Small* by J.B. Phillips. I tried to imagine God bigger. Our human concepts of time, space, and particle physics lead us toward infinity; is it such a jump to believe that we are surrounded by eternity?

I saw a vision of God creating a universe, writing the laws of both quantum physics and relativity theory—a God even capable of creating other universes with other laws. I envisioned the mind of God, the unfathomable, immense mind of God, the ultimate Creator whose thoughts become our reality.

And in this mind of God, I am a thought. His thought. His creation. I may be infinitely tiny compared to the grandeur and complexity of the universe, but still I am a purposeful thought in the mind of God. And if we are surrounded by eternity, is not existence in the mind of God a kind of heaven in itself?

That was my Good Friday vision. Life has purpose because God has created me. I am his thought now and into eternity.

That was when my depression lifted. I was ready for resurrection. I was ready for Easter morning.

A*s Jesus and his disciples were leaving Jericho, a large crowd followed him. Two blind men were sitting by the roadside, and when they heard that Jesus was passing by, they shouted, "Lord, Son of David, have mercy on us!"*

The crowd rebuked them and told them to be quiet, but they shouted all the louder, "Lord, Son of David, have mercy on us!"

Jesus stopped and called to them. "What do you want me to do for you?" he asked.

"Lord," they answered, "we want our sight."

Jesus had compassion on them and touched their eyes. Immediately they received their sight and followed him (Matt. 20:29-34).

This sounds familiar. In Matt. 9:27-31, our Miracle #8, two blind men follow Jesus, calling out for his mercy. Now two more blind men wait at a roadside making the same request. There are four differences in this second story:

1. The blind men add the term *Lord* to their address "Son of David."

2. Jesus asks the first pair, but not the second, for a statement of belief before he heals them.

3. Jesus admonishes the first pair, but not the second, to keep their healing experience a secret.

4. The first pair, or their friends and relatives, against Jesus's request, spread the news about him all over the region, while the second pair got up and followed Jesus.

There are different kinds of blindness. There is the common type in which the brain, through a fault in the eyes or the optic nerves and tracts, becomes unaware of environmental electromagnetic signals in the visual spectrum.

There is another kind of blindness in which the soul becomes unaware of the light that is creation and life and eternity. The inevitable disability, decay, and death of our physical existence become the soul's only reality.

None of us has the power to cure our own blindness. We don't know what we can't see. But when we sit quietly in the darkness, we can hear a celebration passing by, and some-

thing deep within us cries out to the Light of the universe
—*Lord, have mercy on us.*

Jesus had compassion on two blind beggars in Jericho, and he had compassion on two blind souls in Jacksonville. We all got up and followed him, because there was no place we would rather be than in his footsteps and in his presence.

You, too, if you are sitting in the darkness, may hear a celebration passing by. If you do, I urge you to cry out to the Lord of the universe for mercy. He will have compassion. And you will follow him to see an amazing universe.

14

THE 14TH MIRACLE

I know. You have just flipped to the cover to be sure the title said "thirteen." But here is a fourteenth miracle, so I owe you an explanation. The last thirteen miracles covered all the individual healings described in the book of Matthew. This chapter is different. This is about those of us who have been entrusted with the healing of others and have found that we're coming up short of the bar we have set for ourselves. Just because the wounds are self-inflicted does not mean they hurt any less; they hurt more. We feel like "it would be better if we had not been born" to paraphrase the passage below. The fourteenth miracle is about hope for the healer.

"The one who has dipped his hand into the bowl with me will betray me. The Son of Man will go just as it is written about him. But woe to that man who betrays the Son of Man! It would be better for him if he had not been born (Matt. 26:23).

. . .

I n the early 1980's I cared for a forty-eight year-old man with an acute subarachnoid hemorrhage from aneurysm. In those days, delaying surgery for seven days after the initial bleed was thought to allow time for the brain swelling to go down, making the surgery safer. The decreased surgical mortality made up for the small number of people who would re-bleed during the waiting period. One of the trickiest parameters to manage during that week was blood pressure. If the pressure went too high, the aneurysm would rupture; if the pressure went too low, the patient would suffer a stroke.

This man's high blood pressure was difficult to control on several medicines. Fearing a rupture any moment, I ordered a seldom-used IV alpha-blocker at a low-test dosage of 0.5 mg. Normal doses would be 1 to 2 mg. An hour after the phone call, the patient went into shock and the ICU staff began resuscitation. I arrived at the hospital a few minutes later to help with what turned out to be an unsuccessful code.

The fatal blood pressure drop had occurred shortly after the "test" dose. The nurse held out the empty 5.0 mg glass vial. She had given ten times the ordered dose, a lethal mistake.

They don't make that drug anymore, and pharmaceutical companies now take care to avoid packaging medicines in ways that make such mistakes easy. But the changes came too late for that patient, and too late for that nurse.

She was inconsolable.

We make mistakes. She read a drug label wrong. Judas Iscariot read the Messiah wrong, and no one has ever forgotten his betrayal with a kiss. I know I've made big mistakes. A drill plunging into the all-important speech and language areas as I tried to drain a subdural hematoma. An injury to the carotid artery leading to a fatal stroke while I tried to get control of blood flow to a giant aneurysm. A wrong-sided scalp incision. A bruised spinal cord.

The consequences of the big mistake are not limited to the victim. Yes, the nurse's patient died. But what happened to the nurse? She was a good nurse—smart, hard working, and compassionate. When we lost the patient, did we lose the nurse too?

Yes, Jesus died. But what happened to Judas?

W*hen Judas, who had betrayed him, saw that Jesus was condemned, he was seized with remorse and returned the thirty silver coins to the chief priests and elders. "I have sinned," he said, "for I have betrayed innocent blood."*

"What is that to us?" they replied. "That's your responsibility."

So Judas threw the money into the temple and left. Then he went away and hanged himself (Matt. 27:3-5).

R emorse leads to despair. Returning the money is not enough. Despair leads to suicide.

The nurse underwent a review and received a cautionary letter in her permanent file. She took a course in error prevention. The drug company changed the way they packaged the medicine, and the hospital changed risky methods of ordering and dispensing medicines. She could have returned to working in the ICU, but she did not. She needed one more thing to be fully restored.

I know. There are times when the word *sorry* is too small.

I've paid for the consequences of my own mistakes, struggled with my own self-confidence, wondered if I should go back the next day to take care of the next sick person.

The passion story of Jesus carries a parallel story of betrayal. Judas wasn't the only one to lose hope. Peter, in spite of his bluster of faithfulness on the night of the arrest —*even if I have to die with you I will never disown you,* he said —by morning had indeed publicly denied knowing Jesus three times. When the cock crowed at the break of dawn, Peter remembered his vow and wept.

Matthew doesn't mention Peter again in his Gospel. Neither does Mark. Luke and John both tell us Peter ran to the tomb Easter morning after two women had found it empty. Then we don't hear anything about Peter until another episode a few weeks later is recounted in the Gospel of John.

Peter had given up Jerusalem, returned to his home and his old job. I imagine him severely depressed. He had stood at the threshold of the Kingdom of Heaven, looked in, saw the endless beauty, and met the king. Then someone asked if he knew him, and Peter said, *No, no, no. Not me!* Then, three days later, his own eyes told him that he was wrong. Jesus was who he said he was, and Peter had failed his very first trial.

Three years before, when Jesus had sent the disciples out on their own for the first time, in his guidance had said, "Whoever disowns me before others, I will disown before my Father in heaven."

Peter disowned Jesus and now was disowned himself before the Father in heaven. Life could offer him nothing more than a return to fishing in the obscure province of Galilee. He had turned away from the kingdom of heaven at the critical moment. He had made the big mistake.

Now he worked all night and caught not one fish. No longer was he even good at fishing, a total and complete failure. And this time of day was the worst, the graying of the sky before dawn, the time the cock crows. Tired, depressed, and hungry, he felt like throwing himself overboard.

In a few minutes he would do just that. But for a reason he did not expect.

He smelled something. Smoke. And fried fish and warm bread. It tickled his hunger and made him lift his head. A hundred yards away a small fire flickered on shore. Some early riser getting ready to make breakfast. Some early riser who was apparently a better fisherman.

"Friend," the stranger called out to them, "haven't you any fish?"

Was their failure that obvious? Even from a hundred yards away?

Peter's companions shouted back, "No."

"Throw your net on the right side of the boat and you will find some."

Just what he needed— a know-it-all, an idiot bent on making them all look like idiots. Like the water on one side was different than the water on the other. Before he could say a word, though, their nets were up and tossed out again over the opposite gunwale.

The net filled quickly, and the boat tipped dangerously starboard. They couldn't pull in the seine of squiggling fish. Peter's crew kept the ropes tight and started rowing for shore, dragging their catch.

Peter squinted through the mist and the predawn gray at the flame and the figure on the shore. It sounded like, looked like . . . but it couldn't be. Then his cousin John whispered loud enough that Peter heard—*the Lord*.

He looked back into the boat. James and Andrew strug-

gled with the oars. Thomas and Nathaniel kept the net tight;
John minded the tiller while the other two tried to coax a
breeze into the sail. Peter should have helped: the boat
barely made headway, and he was clearly the strongest
rower. John lifted his eyes from his struggles long enough to
meet his gaze. *The Lord*, he mouthed.

Peter leapt over the side, the cold water shocking his
tired mind bright and clear. He swam hard and fast, keeping
his eyes on the small flame. Dripping across the beach he
came to the banks of flaming coals, fish already cooking and
bread being warmed.

Jesus (it had to be Jesus) said nothing at first, only
squatted by the fire and turned the fish. Peter, too, said nothing. What could he say to the man who had talked with
Moses and Elijah, who had walked out of his own tomb?

The words *whoever disowns me* echoed again in Peter's
head, as they had for the last three weeks. Why was Jesus
here, cooking breakfast and giving them fishing instruc-
tions? Was this the final farewell? The final message? *I
warned you, but you wouldn't listen; better luck next time*—he
deserved that message, he knew he did. What he didn't
deserve was breakfast and a record-breaking catch.

The boat's keel crunched into the gravel beach behind
him. He heard the bang of the oars on the gunwales and the
splash of men struggling with a full net of live fish.

Finally Jesus stood up. Their eyes met, and Peter waited
for his dismissal. But he said, "Bring some of the fish you
have just caught."

Peter turned and ran to the boat, scrabbling over the
side, grabbing the net from the exhausted crew and dragging it up the beach. They counted one hundred fifty-four
big ones. Then they stood before the fire, Jesus on the other
side with a griddle and a basket of bread. Had the heavens

opened and choirs of angels begun to sing, they would have been less surprised than when he simply said, "Come and have breakfast."

Words failed them. They ate in silent wonder. When they could eat no more, Jesus spoke to Peter. "Do you love me?" he asked.

"Yes, Lord," Peter answered.

Jesus repeated the question two more times; Peter repeated his answer two more times.

Three times Peter denied knowing Jesus; three times Peter affirmed loving Jesus. The balance was restored. Jesus went on to say a few more things, saving the most important for last: "Follow me."

After the big mistake, you can throw the coins back into the temple, you can take your letters of reprimand and remedial education courses and pay your fines. You can say you're sorry.

But if the mistake is big enough, you still live in the cloud of despair.

I hope you haven't made any big mistakes. Some of us have divorced someone that didn't deserve it. Some of us have abandoned children; some of us have had abortions. Some of us have robbed people legally or illegally. Some of us have killed people for no good reason, and some for a good reason only to discover there are no good reasons.

Remorse, depression, and despair pull us into a deep, dark place. If you are there right now, remember—that little light you see a long distance off in the mist is Jesus cooking breakfast for you.

Head for shore. He will heal you. You will live again in peace and joy.

That is the greatest miracle of all.

NOTES

Introduction

1. Matt. 4:17 (NIV; all subsequent citations are from this version)
2. Matt. 4:23

ACKNOWLEDGMENTS

Mary Lohse has the eyes of a reader, the mind of a writer, and the heart of wisdom; without her I am lost.

I would also like to thank the many readers of the website posts who encouraged me to write this book.

The final production of this book would not be possible without Nancy Stone for her invaluable editorial assistance and John Wollinka for his cover art.

Behind the scenes, Ansley Goodrich Ward provided not only the author photo but invaluable guidance and encouragement, and Robert Bellinger provided much needed website creation and maintenance.

ALSO BY DEAN C. LOHSE, MD

<u>The Surgeon's Sin–Atonement</u>

A novel. Neurosurgeon Peter Jenson botches a brain tumor operation. With his patient dying, his wife leaving, and his enemies denouncing his ability to practice, he begins the long journey to redemption by making a promise he shouldn't keep to a woman he can't refuse, and seeking the help he needs from a man he can't trust.

The journey leads to anxious surgeries in Florida and gunfights in Central America, resulting only in despair. Finally, Peter makes a mutual survival pact with his friend's widow, a suicidal alcoholic. Together they seek a path of love and forgiveness as he faces the fulfillment of a fatal promise, an act that may cost him everything.

ebook links: The Surgeon's Sin